True Freedom

True Freedom

Spinoza's Practical Philosophy

Brent Adkins

LEXINGTON BOOKS
A division of

ROWMAN & LITTLEFIELD PUBLISHERS, INC.
Lanham • Boulder • New York • Toronto • Plymouth, UK

LEXINGTON BOOKS

A division of Rowman & Littlefield Publishers, Inc.
A wholly owned subsidary of The Rowman & Littlefield Publishing Group, Inc.
4501 Forbes Boulevard, Suite 200
Lanham, MD 20706

Estover Road
Plymouth PL6 7PY
United Kingdom

British Library Cataloguing in Publication Information Available

Library of Congress Cataloging-in-Publication Data

Adkins, Brent, 1969–
  True freedom : Spinoza's practical philosophy / Brent Adkins.
      p. cm.
  Includes bibliographical references and index.
  ISBN 978-0-7391-3939-4 (cloth : alk. paper)
  ISBN 978-0-7391-3940-0 (pbk. : alk. paper)
  ISBN 978-0-7391-3941-7 (electronic)
  1. Spinoza, Benedictus de, 1632–1677. 2. Liberty. 3. Life. 4. Ethics. I. Title.
  B3998.A35 2009
  199".492 — dc22   2009023963

Printed in the United States of America

For Aubrey and Bauer

Sed omnia praeclara tam difficilia, quam rara sunt.

Contents

Acknowledgments

Even though this book bears only one name, all books are collaborative efforts. These collaborations take place in numerous ways on numerous levels. I would like to acknowledge some of those collaborations here.

To begin with, this book has been greatly supported by Roanoke College, not only through a sabbatical leave in the fall of 2008, but through a Faculty Scholars Grant beginning in 2007, which freed up some much needed time for research. Additionally, Roanoke College has been generous in supporting travel to numerous conferences and speaking engagements.

My colleagues in the department of religion and philosophy have also been remarkably generous in their willingness to read and discuss what I've written. Ned Wisnefske read and commented on portions of this manuscript, and I've had numerous fruitful discussions with Monica Vilhauer, who is always unfailing in the generosity and precision of her questions. Gerry McDermott was an invaluable resource in putting together a prospectus that would be attractive to a press. Finally, Paul Hinlicky went above and beyond the call of duty by reading the entire manuscript and helpfully commenting on it.

Given the aims of the book, it would not be possible in its present form without all the students that I've discussed Spinoza with. The biggest group is no doubt the hundreds of students who've been in my Values and the Responsible Life course. Teaching Spinoza to a class with no philosophical background has been a great proving ground for many of the ideas found here, and these ideas are better for having gone through this crucible. I would be remiss, though, if I didn't also mention the students from Philosophy and Film and Environmental Philosophy, who allowed me to try different and broader approaches to Spinoza.

I would also like to single out two students who were instrumental in the process of writing this book. First, Beth Nicoll helpfully tracked down references and commented on the opening chapter. Second, Dana Mueller read the entire manuscript multiple times and never failed to give perspicacious comments.

In September 2007, I was able to present the basic ideas that inform the book at the Washington State University–University of Idaho Philosophy Colloquium. I'm grateful to Aaron Bunch for his kind invitation and to the faculties and graduate students for their helpful comments. Chapter 8 was presented to the International Social Theory Consortium in May 2009. I would also like to thank Laura Hengehold, who read and commented on the complete manuscript.

Matt McAdam has been a great resource at Rowman and Littlefield and I'm thankful for his support in getting this project published. I would also like to thank their anonymous reviewer for the helpful and encouraging comments.

As always my professional accomplishments would be impossible without the love and support of my family. This book is dedicated to them.

Introduction
Spinoza: A User's Guide

My primary interest in Spinoza is not as a professional philosopher, although I think that philosophically Spinoza has a great deal to offer. My interest is straightforwardly practical. I am convinced that Spinoza's greatest value lies in his ability to describe what it means to live well and to offer a path toward that goal. Of course, living well for Spinoza is inseparable from doing philosophy, but doing philosophy is never a dry academic exercise. It is the pursuit of what is best in us, an understanding of who we are and our place in the world.

The chief issue for Spinoza in living well is action, but not in the sense of judging whether a particular act is right or wrong. This kind of judgment is available, but it is secondary to Spinoza's concern about the difference between activity and passivity. To put the matter as succinctly as possible, we are living well, or we are truly free, only when we are active. In contrast to this, we are not living well when we are passive. The key to understanding Spinoza is knowing the difference. While in an abstract sense it is easy to distinguish between the active and passive, the terms are simply opposed to one another. In practice this distinction is not always clear. As we'll see, everything hinges on the emotions, our way of engaging with the world. Some emotions are active. Some are passive. One of the tasks of this book is to clearly articulate the difference between the active and the passive, not only in regard to individuals but also in regard to politics, religion, and the environment.

The bottom line for Spinoza is that action of any kind can only follow from understanding, while passivity at bottom follows from a failure to understand. Not only do I need to understand myself, but I need to understand the world around me in order to act. Spinoza is not unique in the history of philosophy in recognizing the connection between understanding and action. The wisdom traditions across all cultures are replete with this connection from Buddhism to Judaism to the Ancient Greeks. Thus one of the tasks of the book is to show Spinoza's continuity with other traditions where it is illuminating, but more importantly to show where he is bringing something new to the discussion. As we'll see, what Spinoza brings that's new to the discussion is freedom.

Unfortunately, Spinoza's connection with the ancient wisdom traditions is often lost in focusing exclusively on his claims about the nature of the universe, his metaphysics, and his claims about the nature of knowledge, his epistemology. My first encounter with Spinoza occurred as an undergraduate in an introductory philosophy course. In the flood of all the other philosophers and ideas, I can't say that Spinoza made a particularly strong impression. I remember words like "substance" and "pantheism" being thrown around liberally but not much else. I didn't encounter Spinoza again until I was a graduate student in philosophy, although in the meantime through osmosis, I was able to put together a few more of the contours of his thought and his relation to the history of philosophy. Like most people I was put off by his style, which often reads like a recipe for a dish no one would be interested in eating, even though there was also something compelling about it. What remained opaque to me was how the *Ethics* was an ethics at all. Because Spinoza is usually taught as part of a survey course known as Modern Western Philosophy, the primary focus of these courses is these thinkers' theories of reality and knowledge. This focus, while valuable, gives short shrift to any other views, particularly ethical views, these thinkers might have had.

My encounter with Spinoza as an ethical thinker did not occur until several years later when I was tasked to teach an ethics course. It was my first ethics course and my immediate inclination was to teach it historically. I had already lined up most of the usual suspects for such a course, Aristotle, Kant, Mill, and Nietzsche, but I felt it was missing something from the modern period (as seventeenth- and eighteenth-century philosophy is inexplicably called) and something from the twentieth century. I filled in the twentieth-century gap with Levinas, and without knowing what I was getting into, put Spinoza on the syllabus. I was woefully unprepared to teach Spinoza to undergraduates, especially the ethical parts of Spinoza, since my familiarity ended with his theories of reality and knowledge. Like a good academic, I went to the library for some help and was fortunate enough to stumble across Stuart Hampshire's *Two Theories of Morality*. The book, now sadly out of print, did me the great service of not only explaining what exactly was ethical about Spinoza's writings but to compare Spinoza's views to Aristotle's, someone I was much more familiar with. It was at this point that the conviction began to grow in me that Spinoza not only made important claims about ethics but that those claims were relevant today. As Hampshire makes clear, Spinoza's view of the universe has much more in common with contemporary scientific accounts of the universe. More importantly Spinoza's ethics follow directly from his view of the universe. As a result there is a very satisfying holism to Spinoza's philosophy. One is not required to believe one thing about the way the universe works and another thing about the way ethics work. They both work the same, each a part of a seamless garment.

The most important thing that I've learned from students about Spinoza is that they won't slog through the theories of reality and knowledge to get the prize at the end of Spinoza's *Ethics*. When it comes to Spinoza we start with dessert. I've adopted that same strategy here. I begin with what I take to be Spinoza's fundamental ethical insight that we get carried away by harmful emotions when we do not properly understand the situation. Or, to the degree that we understand, harmful emotions are dissipated and replaced by helpful ones. Of course, at this point we have more questions than answers. What does it mean to "properly understand"? How are harmful and helpful emotions distinguished? By what process are emotions dissipated and replaced?

Answering these questions does require that we engage with Spinoza's theories of reality and knowledge, but this will all be in the service of understanding what makes Spinoza's ethics tick. My goal here is the same as it is with my students: to show that this strange thinker from the seventeenth century remains eminently practical today. Although other commentators on Spinoza have referred to this passage before, it is still apt. Bernard Malamud's *The Fixer* tells the story of a man who comes across Spinoza's *Ethics* and is asked about its effects before a judge:

"Let me ask you what brought you to Spinoza? Is it that he was a Jew?"

"No, your honor. I didn't know who or what he was when I first came across the book—they don't exactly love him in the synagogue, if you've read the story of his life. I found it in a junkyard in a nearby town, paid a kopek and left cursing myself for wasting money hard to come by. Later I read through a few pages and kept on going as though there were a whirlwind at my back. As I say, I didn't understand every word but when you're dealing with such ideas you feel as though you were taking a witch's ride. After that I wasn't the same man."

"Would you mind explaining what you think Spinoza's work means? In other words if it's a philosophy what does it state?"

"That's not so easy to say. . . . The book means different things according to the subject of the chapters, though it's all united underneath. But what I think it means is that he was out to make a free man of himself—as much as one can according to his philosophy, if you understand my meaning—by thinking things through and connecting everything up, if you'll go along with that, your honor."[1]

Notice that the man in the story zeroes in on the ethical import of Spinoza's work. After reading the whole thing, even if he didn't understand all of it, he saw that the key to Spinoza's philosophy lies in his conception of freedom. As we will see, Spinoza's idea of freedom is radically different from what we generally suppose. Furthermore, his idea of freedom is not limited to individual freedom but extends to politics and religion as well. The reason for this is that for Spinoza "it's all united underneath."

There has been an explosion of interest in Spinoza over the past few years, a new biography, historical studies of his relation to his contemporaries, as well as memoirs and a monumental study of Spinoza's impact on the European Enlightenment. My goal here is much more modest. I do not pursue biographical or historical detail so that I can explicate Spinoza's arguments on their own terms. My task in short is to show how Spinoza made a free man out of himself and how he proposes to make us free as well.

NOTES

1. Bernard Malamud, *The Fixer* (New York: Farrar, Straus, and Giroux, 2004). Quoted in Gilles Deleuze, *Spinoza: Practical Philosophy*, translated by Robert Hurley (San Francisco: City Lights, 1988), 1.

Chapter 1
The Curious Incident of
the Rude Driver in the SUV

While I was living in Chicago, I developed an unfortunate case of road rage. It seemed as if everywhere I went, I was beset on all sides by either incompetent or thoughtless (and thus incompetent) drivers. A drive through any part of the city was the catalyst for the most astonishing phrases coming out of my mouth. I became capable of swearing in numerous languages and learned the appropriate, accompanying hand gestures. While no one was spared my wrath, I reserved a special hatred for the drivers of SUVs. Their incompetence seemed magnified by the ridiculous size of their vehicles. Not only did the SUVs take up too much space, but their drivers did not see the point of slowing down during rain or snow. They often parallel parked poorly, not closing the gap to the next car or ending up too far from the curb. It also rankled me that if there were an accident, though it would no doubt be the fault of the SUV driver, I, in my compact car, would surely be killed, while the SUV driver would walk away unscathed. I was convinced that justice on the road was impossible.

Imagine that while driving in this state of mind (courteously and mindfully, of course) I see out of the corner of my eye a very large object coming toward me very quickly. I slam on my brakes to avoid a collision. As it passes me I see that it is my sworn enemy, the SUV. As I honk my horn, a fusillade of expletives erupts from my mouth. The SUV never deviates from its path. There are no break lights, no I'm-sorry-I'm-an-idiot wave from the driver, no acknowledgment of any kind. I am livid. At this point, I begin to construct a lyrical and cinematic revenge fantasy.

In my fantasy I speed up in front of the SUV and skid sideways blocking the lane. The angry driver gets out of his car to give me a piece of his mind. I, too, step out of my car and I've been magically transformed. First, everything begins happening in slow motion. Second, my clothes have changed from the drab earth tones that I usually wear into all black. Suddenly, I no longer need glasses and am able to wear exceedingly cool sunglasses. In short I look very much like a character from the *Matrix* movies. I am revenge personified. The SUV driver is unfazed by this and continues angrily walking toward me. When I round the back of my car he stops in horror and begins to run the other way, because it's only then that he sees the sawed-off, pump-action 12-gauge shotgun that has been concealed by my black trench coat, which is artfully flapping in the wind. Grim-faced and without saying a word I begin blowing large holes in the tires and radiator of the SUV, no doubt ensuring that this SUV will never endanger anyone again.

I am brought out of my reverie just before uttering some witty quip such as, "License revoked" or "Looks like you need a tune-up." The SUV and I happen to be going in the same direction, but it now appears to be turning. My hope is to get in an icy stare of moral superiority before he drives off, never to be seen again. Luckily for him, he is spared the horror of my wrathful gaze as he turns down a different street and pulls immediately into a parking lot. I see that it is a hospital parking lot and that he has pulled up to the emergency room doors. He quickly gets out and runs to the other side of the SUV to open the door and help out a very pregnant woman.

Numerous feelings pass through me at that moment, nausea, guilt, embarrassment, shame, and an overwhelming, "Oh . . . so that's why he cut me off." One feeling that does not pass through me, though, is anger. The lack of anger at this point seems remarkable. The anger was something I had been laying the groundwork on for years. I had been slowly and carefully nurturing it, judiciously recording all the slights against me. I had localized the source of my anger in SUVs, and then all the elements came together in such a way as to insure an explosive reaction that left me constructing an exquisitely detailed revenge fantasy. All of this was gone in an instant. Why? The first thing that probably comes to mind is that I no longer had a reason to be angry. Or, perhaps, I felt that driving a pregnant woman in labor to the hospital was an acceptable reason to be cut off. Or, maybe, I saw that my anger was based on a misconception. I assumed that the driver of the SUV cut me off because he was incompetent or thoughtless. Once I saw, however, that he was neither incompetent nor thoughtless, the anger based on that assumption dissolved.

As we move through Spinoza's philosophy we'll be able to give an increasingly precise account of exactly what happened there, but even at this point I think we can see what I take to be Spinoza's fundamental ethical insight. Provisionally, we could state Spinoza's insight this way: To the degree that one understands, one cannot be angry. While this insight captures what happens in the illustration, it also raises more questions than it answers. On the one hand, it is certainly helpful to reduce the amount of anger in the world. That in itself would seem to have numerous positive effects. On the other hand, does Spinoza's ethics only deal with anger? Does it have anything to say about other emotions? Is it *only* about the emotions? Also, what precisely does it mean to "understand" in this case? Isn't my understanding in the case of the SUV driver pure happenstance? What if I never discovered that I was cut off for justifiable reasons? What if the SUV driver is in fact thoughtless and incompetent? Is my anger justified, then? What about the other emotions that accompanied my understanding, the guilt and shame? Why do these arise?

Obviously, we do not yet have the resources to respond to these questions. The primary purpose of the illustration is to show that at least in some cases, when we know why something happened we are much less likely to get angry about it. Or, even better, if we find ourselves angry about something and then learn why it happened, our anger dissipates. We'll have to look very closely at Spinoza to see if this model can be generalized. Furthermore, we'll have to examine precisely what can be generalized. What we'll discover is that Spinoza has a full-blown theory of the emotions that follows from his more abstract claims about God and the mind, and that the relation between the understanding and the emotions extends far beyond anger. Spinoza says it this way, "An affect which is a passion ceases to be a passion as soon as we form a clear and distinct idea of it."[1] There are a few things that we can note at this point. First, notice that Spinoza uses the word "affect" to refer to what we would normally call "emotion." This is because Spinoza is concerned about all of the ways in which we affect and are affected by our environment. These ways of affecting and being affected, although they include the emotions, are in fact much broader than the emotions. Thus being angry for Spinoza is an affect, but so is stubbing my toe or any of the innumerable ways that I interact with the world around me. The second thing we can note about Spinoza's proposition is that what concerns him is the type of affect one is experiencing, namely the passions. What Spinoza has in mind here is not captured by the word's connection with a related word like "passionate." The passions for Spinoza are not primarily the things we are passionate about, that is, the things that we pursue with the most vigor and energy. Rather, the principal connotation operative in Spinoza's use of "passion" is "passive." The passions, for Spinoza, are thus the ways in which we are affected that render us passive. To be passive for Spinoza is to not be myself, to be controlled by something other than me. We have a ways to go before we see why this is, but for Spinoza passive affects are the source of all detrimental behavior.

The final thing we can note about Spinoza's proposition is that if passive affects are the source of all detrimental behavior, the solution is forming clear and distinct ideas. Spinoza is clearly echoing Descartes in his use of the phrase "clear and distinct," and in many ways each has the same thing in mind. What is at the forefront of both Spinoza's and Descartes' minds here is something that cannot be doubted, or something bordering on transparency or full disclosure. With this in mind, let's return briefly to the run-in with the SUV driver. When I was cut off by the SUV driver I became angry and reveled in revenge fantasies. Was I passive at this point? It seems that I was. All of my thoughts and actions were suddenly dependent on the SUV driver. I was no longer controlling myself; I was being

controlled by something other than me. This is the very definition of "passive."
At what point was I released from my passivity? At the point that I understood
why the driver cut me off. When the driver's reasons for acting the way he did
became apparent to me, I was no longer angry. That is, when I clearly and dis-
tinctly understood why I was cut off, I was no longer affected passively. A clear
and distinct idea replaced a passion.

The replacement of passive affects by clear and distinct ideas succinctly describes
the mechanics of Spinoza's ethical theory, but in order to get a sense of the theory as
a whole I'd like to look at the way that Spinoza concludes the *Ethics*. Perhaps, then,
if we see where Spinoza is heading we can better understand the steps required to
get there. In the closing comments to his final proposition Spinoza's language is
reminiscent of the wisdom literature in the Hebrew Bible. In the opening two chapters of *Proverbs*, Wisdom personified lays out two possible paths, the path of folly
and the path of wisdom. Wisdom portrays herself as calling out in vain,

> How long, O naïve ones, will you love simplicity?
> And scoffers delight themselves in scoffing,
> And fools hate knowledge?[2]

Those who fail to heed her call will reap the reward of the folly, namely, death.
Let's compare this to what Spinoza says about the ignorant.

> For not only is the ignorant man troubled in many ways by external causes, and un-
> able ever to possess true peace of mind, but he also lives as if he knew neither him-
> self, nor God, nor things; and as soon as he ceases to be acted on, he ceases to be.[3]

For Spinoza, those who remain ignorant are never really themselves. Their
lives are a series of passive affects, being controlled by things other than them.

On the other hand, those who heed the call of Wisdom, according to *Proverbs*,
will be greatly rewarded.

> Make your ear attentive to wisdom,
> Incline your heart to understanding;
> For if you cry for discernment,
> Lift your voice for understanding;
> If you seek her as silver,
> And search for her as for hidden treasures;
> Then you will discern the fear of the Lord,
> And discover the knowledge of God.[4]

In a similar contrast, Spinoza writes this about the wise,

> On the other hand, the wise man, insofar as he is considered as such, is hardly troubled
> in spirit, but being, by a certain eternal necessity, conscious of himself, and of God, and
> of things, he never ceases to be, but always possesses true peace of mind.[5]

Spinoza's ethical theory is thus about two possible paths one might follow, two fundamentally opposed ways of affecting and being affected. One path leads away from peace and knowledge and toward death. The other path leads toward peace and knowledge and away from death. Also, notice that Spinoza's concerns are characterized in terms that would be familiar to anyone. He takes up the ancient philosophical dictum of "Know yourself." He takes up the theological concern, knowledge of God, that had been dominant in Europe for the previous millennia and a half and is evidenced in the much older tradition of Hebrew wisdom literature that Spinoza would have been intimately familiar with. Finally, he takes up the contemporary scientific concern of knowing the world. The wise person possesses knowledge of all of these things and thus possesses the concomitant peace of mind. The ignorant person, however, does not possess this knowledge and thus fails to achieve peace of mind.

After laying out these two paths, Spinoza concludes the *Ethics* on an edifying note:

> If the way I have shown to lead to these things now seems very hard, still, it can be found. And of course, what is found so rarely must be hard. For if salvation were at hand, and could be found without great effort, how could nearly everyone neglect it? But all things excellent are as difficult as they are rare.[6]

The tone here remains very similar to the passages from *Proverbs*. It is patently obvious to the writer of *Proverbs* and Spinoza that the world is lacking in wisdom, and yet few people are actively seeking it. Furthermore, although it is clearly advantageous to possess wisdom, it is difficult to achieve. The rewards, however, are extensive. The writer of *Proverbs* speaks in terms of "deliverance," deliverance from "the way of evil" and all the things to be found on it, from the one who "speaks perversely," from the ones who "walk in the ways of darkness," from the one whose "tracks lead to the dead."[7] Spinoza adopts a Christian idiom and speaks of "salvation" as the reward for following the path of wisdom. We'll return to Spinoza's use of religious language in chapter 9.

As we have seen there are numerous resonances between Spinoza's project and numerous intellectual and religious traditions. As we progress through Spinoza's thought these resonances will become richer and increase in complexity. One famous commentator on Spinoza's *Ethics* went so far as to say that everything in the *Ethics* has already been said but that Spinoza puts it together into an absolutely unique system.[8] Thus, while we will see numerous points of convergence between Spinoza's ethical theory and Stoicism, Epicureanism, Aristotelianism, Cartesiansim, Christianity, and Judaism, our primary focus will be to highlight what differentiates Spinoza from these other traditions.

One crucial point of differentiation between Spinoza and most ethical theories lies in the descriptive nature of Spinoza's ethics. Most ethical theories are prescriptive rather than descriptive. To be prescriptive means that a particular way of life or particular act are prescribed, or required of a person. Prescriptive ethics are usually articulated in terms of "ought" or "should." For example, a prescriptive ethics would say things like, "One ought not lie," or "One should always help others." Depending on the ethical theory, numerous reasons will be given for why one ought or ought not do something or live a certain way.

Some (utilitarians or consequentialists) argue that "ought" is determined by the greatest good. That is, one should do that which produces the greatest good and refrain from doing what does not. Others (deontologists or Kantians) argue that "ought" is not determined by the consequences but by whether or not the principle one is acting on entails a contradiction. The utilitarian position is much more straightforward, but both positions can be illustrated using the same example. If we pose the ethical question, "Is it wrong to lie?" we're already asking in terms of prescriptive ethics. What we really want to know is, which actions are approved and which are forbidden. Both consequentialists and deontologists are eager to oblige us here. Both would say that it is wrong to lie, but both would say it is wrong for different reasons. The consequentialist would say that it is usually wrong to lie, because lying tends to decrease the general welfare. In short, we shouldn't lie, because lying leads to bad consequences. The deontologist, on the other hand, would say that lying is wrong, not because it produces bad consequences, but because it is inherently wrong. Even if one could imagine a situation in which lying produced good consequences, this would not overcome the inherent immorality of lying.

In contrast to the prescriptive ethics of utilitarianism and deontology, Spinoza's ethics is purely descriptive. While prescriptive ethics are predicated on imperatives—one must . . . , one is duty bound to . . . , one ought to . . . —Spinoza's ethics is predicated on conditional or causal claims. *If* you follow the path of wisdom, the result will be life. *If* you follow the path of ignorance, the result will be death. It is important, though, not to see the consequent of each of these conditionals as a reward or punishment imposed externally. For Spinoza there is no final judgment whereby one is deemed to have followed the path of wisdom or ignorance. Rather, following the path of wisdom is its own reward and following the path of ignorance is its own punishment. Spinoza imagines the path of wisdom to be like eating wholesome food and the path of ignorance like eating poison. It's not as if after a lifetime of eating healthy food an external authority would then arrive and say, "You have eaten well your whole life, you are now granted the reward of health." No, health is simply a function of eating well. If I eat well, I *am* healthy. By the same token, the necessary effect of eating poison is death (or at the very least grave illness). I can't expect to eat poison with impunity my whole life only at the end to be judged not worthy of health. Insofar as poison is inherently opposed to my health, the ingestion of it leads away from health.[9] Spinoza's ethical theory is descriptive in precisely this sense. He is concerned to show the conditions under which one could be considered as living well, wisely, and the conditions under which one could be considered as living poorly, foolishly. This living well or poorly, however, is not an external judgment given at the end of life, it is the causally necessary effect of one's actions.

In order to flesh out this conception of ethics, we'll need a much more fully realized account of Spinoza's theories of human nature and action. In a preliminary way, though, we can characterize Spinoza's ethics as an experimentalism. It is common to contrast the ethical theories of the Ancients and Moderns in this way: Ancient discourse on ethics was guided by the fundamental question, "How should one live?" This question led to concerns about the whole of life, which in turn led to concerns about character development (i.e., virtue). Their reasoning worked like this: A person can only live well insofar as he or she is using reason, because reason is what differentiates us from other creatures. However, using reason requires education and practice. That is, one must *become* the type of creature that reasons. The process of learning and habituation required to become a rational animal is the character development called "virtue" by the Ancients.

In contrast to this, the ethical (or, more properly moral) theory of the Moderns is dominated by the question, "How should one act?" Notice the shift in emphasis here. The primary emphasis is no longer on one's whole life, although this is not entirely absent from the Moderns. Rather, the emphasis is on judging particular acts. In general, this type of moral theorizing takes the form of articulating a principle, and then deciding whether a particular act violates this principle or is in conformity with it.

Given this contrast between the Ancients and Moderns, it seems clear that Spinoza has much more in common with the Ancients. Indeed, Michel Foucault argues that Spinoza is the last Ancient philosopher, precisely because he is profoundly concerned with the order and direction of a whole life, what Foucault would call "care of the self," rather than isolated acts.[10] Where Spinoza parts company with both the Ancients and Moderns, though, is the prescriptive nature of their theories. Both are organized by what *ought* to be the case. We saw above that Spinoza's theory is not prescriptive but descriptive. He is not concerned with what ought to be the case but with what *is* the case.

In order to highlight Spinoza's difference from these other types of moral and ethical theorizing, I propose that the question that best organizes Spinoza's ethical theory is, "How *might* one live?" This question is often used as a way of describing much more contemporary ethical theorists such as Friedrich Nietzsche or Gilles Deleuze, but I think it fits quite well with Spinoza's project.[11] Notice that in the shift from "should" in the previous questions to "might" in this question, we shift from prescription to description and from traditional ethics and morals to experimentation. Spinoza recognizes that we are complex creatures capable of interacting with our environment in myriad ways. One of the tasks of Spinoza's philosophy is to understand this complexity and explore its limits. What Spinoza discovers is that some of these interactions are beneficial and some are harmful. Spinoza's second task is to show why these interactions are beneficial or harmful. Finally, Spinoza can show what kind of life one might lead if one interacts with beneficial things. This is the path of wisdom, the path of health, the path of freedom and beatitude. In contrast, Spinoza also shows what kind of life one might lead if one interacts with harmful things. This is the path of ignorance, the path of sickness, the path of curse and bondage.

Spinoza's fundamental ethical insight is that when we understand why something happens it loses its power to control us. When I understood why the SUV driver cut me off, I was no longer angry about it. A great deal of work needs to be done to fully flesh out why this is the case for Spinoza. But, to begin that process we characterized Spinoza's work in terms of the wisdom literature of the Hebrew Bible. Both take very seriously the image of two paths, wisdom and folly. Furthermore, we looked at what distinguished Spinoza from other ethical theories. First, we noted that it was descriptive rather than prescriptive, and finally we noted that it is characterized by a kind of experimentalism. That is, Spinoza is concerned with the possible ways that one might live, which is vast given not only our complexity but the complexity of our environment. In the following chapters we will explore how these fundamental differences set Spinoza apart not only on ethical topics but also wide ranging topics such as psychology, politics, and religion.

NOTES

1. Unless otherwise noted all translations of Spinoza come from *The Collected Works of Spinoza,* vol. 1, edited and translated by Edwin Curley (Princeton: Princeton University Press, 1985). Spinoza's *Ethics* has a standardized citation system that I will employ throughout the remainder of the book. The *Ethics* has five parts, which are indicated in Roman numerals. The part number is followed by the next level of specificity, usually a proposition number. This is indicated by a "P" followed by the number of the proposition as an Arabic numeral. Finally, the citation indicates whether the text is subordinate to the proposition as a demonstration (abbreviated as "D") or a note related to the discussion (indicated with an "S" for "scholia"). The quote above comes from part 5 of the *Ethics* and is proposition 3. Thus, the citation is VP3.

2. Proverbs 1:22. New American Standard Version.

3. VP42S.

4. Proverbs 2:2–5.

5. VP42S.

6. VP42S.

7. Proverbs 2:12–18.

8. Harry Austryn Wolfson, *The Philosophy of Spinoza* (New York: Schocken Books, 1969), 3.

9. Gilles Deleuze, *Spinoza: Practical Philosophy,* translated by Robert Hurley (San Francisco: City Lights, 1998), 22–3.

10. Michel Foucault, *The Hermeneutics of Subject: Lectures at the Collège de France, 1981–1982,* translated by Graham Burchell (New York: Picador, 2005), 27–8.

11. Todd May in his *Gilles Deleuze: An Introduction* (New York: Cambridge University Press, 2005), uses all three of these questions in order to differentiate Deleuze from other modes of thought. Spinoza does not arise in this context, but May does go on to argue that

Chapter 2
What's Love Got to Do with It?

In *The Simpsons* episode, "The Springfield Files," which itself is a spoof of the show the *X-Files*, Homer is convinced that he's seen an extraterrestrial. In the climactic scene the whole town gathers to discover that the "alien" is in fact Mr. Burns, owner of the Springfield nuclear plant. Mr. Burns has been disoriented by drugs and treatments intended to "cheat death for another week" and a "lifetime of working at a nuclear power plant has given him a healthy, green glow." When Mr. Burns appears before the town in this disoriented state he says, "I bring you peace. I bring you love." To which the cigar-smoking Dr. Hibbert retorts, "Is that the kind of love between a man and a woman or between a man and a fine Cuban cigar?"

For the sake of our discussion here, I'll risk killing the comedy by analyzing it. First, if we were to imagine Mr. Burns's response to Dr. Hibbert it would be one of confusion. Mr. Burns is not bringing either of those kinds of love. He would claim to be bringing a more transcendent "love of all humanity" or "love of the universe," as evidenced by the scene closing with the whole town joining hands and singing "Good Morning Starshine" with Leonard Nimoy. Second, both of Dr. Hibbert's examples equate love to a kind of pleasure, sexual or gustatory. (Admittedly, "love between a man and a woman" is ambiguous. It could be the kind of relation that arises in a long-term commitment, but I think it's funnier to imagine Dr. Hibbert responding to Mr. Burns's world-embracing love with the equivalent of, "Is that like the love of sex or the love of smoking?" Maybe it's just me.)

Regardless of how one takes Dr. Hibbert's response, what this short exchange shows is that the word "love" is being used in three distinct ways. How is this possible? On the one hand, when we're asked to reflect on the meaning of "love" we tend toward the more high-minded accounts. We describe love in terms of devotion and sacrifice. Furthermore, we tend to rigorously distinguish love and sex. Sex might be an expression of love, but sex by itself cannot produce love, only lust. Our actual use of the word "love," however, often betrays our high-minded explanation. No one would claim that either Dr. Hibbert or Mr. Burns are misusing the word. In fact, it's the collision of these opposed meanings that make the exchange humorous. We do say things like, "I love these shoes," or "I love this TV show." I can say that I love my wife, my kids, and Italian food without having to use scare quotes at any point to indicate that I'm using the word ironically or in opposition to its appropriate meaning.

In order to explain what's going on here, I'd like to turn to Spinoza's theory of the affects. In the previous chapter we saw that replacing affects that are passions with clear and distinct ideas is crucial to Spinoza's ethical theory, but it's not entirely clear at this point what the affects are and why some of them might be passions. Also, the existence of affects as passions raises the possibility of affects that are not passions. Suffice it to say that Spinoza's theory of the affects is rich and complex, and while it will allow us to answer questions about the nature and definition of the emotions, like love, for example, it also covers much more than the emotions. Spinoza is concerned about the possible ways that we might interact with the rest of the world, from shoes and cigars to other people to the world as a whole.

Spinoza's theory of the affects is found in part III of his *Ethics*. Here Spinoza presents a taxonomy of the types of interactions that one might engage in. He introduces the affects with two remarkable notions. The first is that humans are not a "kingdom within a kingdom." What Spinoza is pointing to here is the relation of humans to the rest of the world. Other theorists of human nature have gone wrong by supposing that the rules governing human interactions are qualitatively different from the rules governing other types of interactions and thus a law unto themselves. As a result, human interactions become deeply mysterious and without precedent. In the face of this mystery all we can do is bemoan our impotence. The mystery of human affects is unsolvable in principle. We cannot understand them, and thus, we are always at their mercy. The best we can do, then, is fulminate with more or less skill against the mysterious vice that afflicts us all. Spinoza's response to this dead end is to argue that there is no qualitative difference between the rules that govern human interactions and the rules that govern other interactions. All interactions share crucial similarities that can be cataloged and, more importantly, understood. For it is only in understanding our affects that we can hope to improve our lot. While Spinoza is adamant that human interactions are not mysteriously different from other types of interactions, he is not claiming that humans are therefore identical to everything else. Humans are manifestly different from other things in the universe. This difference, however, is not the result of the fact that human interactions differ from other interactions. As we will see in a later chapter, human difference emerges from the complex interrelations of the human body not from being a kingdom within a kingdom.

The second remarkable notion by which Spinoza introduces his theory of the affects follows from the first. If humans are not a kingdom within a kingdom, then the rules of their interactions are the same as the rules of other interactions. Human emotions are not opaque. They need to be treated with the same rigor as any other natural phenomenon. As a result human affects are to be treated in the same manner as "lines, planes, and bodies." The reference to geometry here is not accidental. The full title of Spinoza's work is *Ethics, Demonstrated in Geometric Order*. Euclid's *Elements* is clearly in the background here as the model of clarity and logical precision, and Spinoza's style is deeply indebted to Euclid. While to many, Spinoza's style in the *Ethics* is cumbersome and impedes understanding, Spinoza is trying to present his system as clearly as possible. As a result, he doesn't assume any knowledge on the reader's part but clearly defines his terms at the outset. He even goes so far as to articulate truths that he takes to be self-evident, called axioms. For example, "Whatever is, is either in itself or in another."[1] Spinoza takes it as obvious that everything that exists, either depends on something else for its existence (i.e., "in another") or is self-subsistent (i.e., "in itself") and that all objects fit into one of these two categories. Clearly, we are not accustomed to dividing the world in this way, but it does seem to cover all the options, in the same way that, "it is raining or it is not raining outside my window right now" covers all the options regarding precipitation. Spinoza's method then is similar to geometry in that he uses definitions and axioms to construct proofs. Each proof yields a proposition. Propositions can then be combined with other propositions, definitions, and axioms to produce more propositions. The crucial thing for Spinoza is that as in geometry the proofs yield necessary truths, that is, truths that cannot be otherwise. Thus, the propositions deduced in the *Ethics* are for Spinoza on the same order as "the sum of a triangle's interior angles equals the sum of two right angles." This seems reasonable when one is discussing triangles but wholly unreasonable when one is talking about emotions. Is Spinoza saying that there is some sort of formula for love? Furthermore, is he saying that there are necessary conditions for love, and that when these are met, love will always result? As strange as it may sound and as difficult as it may be to believe, yes, that is exactly what Spinoza is saying. He will treat love and any and all other human interactions in the same manner as lines, planes, and solids.

So, Spinoza is not a romantic, but let's reserve judgment about his theory of the emotions until we look at it a little more deeply. Spinoza's theory depends on several interrelated concepts. The first pair comes from the definitions at the beginning of part III: adequate and inadequate cause. What is at issue is the relation between a cause and its effect. Either an effect can be clearly understood through the cause or it cannot. If the effect can be clearly understood through the cause, then it is adequate. If the effect cannot be clearly understood through the cause, then it is inadequate. Much like we saw above in our discussion of axioms, these are exhaustive possibilities for Spinoza. There is no third possibility. All causes are either adequate or inadequate.

In order to illustrate this point, let's suppose that I leave my office to go to the coffee shop down the street. The coffee shop is just a few blocks away, and as

I walk I cross several streets. If at any point, I reflect on my progress and ask, "How did I get here?" My answer, very simply is, "I walked here on my way to the coffee shop." Thus, the effect of my being at any point along the way is understood by the cause of my having walked there on my way somewhere else. Furthermore, the explanation is sufficient. No additional information is needed to explain to anyone the reason why I am at one point on the sidewalk and not another, or why I am walking at all and not in my office. In this case, *I* am the adequate cause of my position.[2]

By way of contrast, let's suppose that as I'm crossing the street on my way to the coffee shop, an SUV runs a stop sign, hits me, and sends me hurtling through space on a trajectory perpendicular to my previous one. If I'm fortunate enough to come to and still enough in possession of my wits to ask, "How did I get here?" The answer can no longer be, "I walked here on my way to the coffee shop." The effect of me lying battered in the middle of the road can no longer be understood solely by my walking to the coffee shop. Thus, I am no longer the adequate cause of my position. Rather, I am the inadequate cause of my position. That is, a complete understanding of the effect requires an account of me *and* my unforeseen collision with the SUV. This distinction between adequate and inadequate causes allows Spinoza to distinguish sharply between activity and passivity. Very succinctly, I act when I am the adequate cause of an effect, and I am passive when I am the inadequate cause of an effect. Thus, in the example above, I was active while walking to the coffee shop under my own power and was passive after being struck by the SUV.

The second set of concepts that are crucial to Spinoza's account of the affects are the three basic affects joy, sadness, and striving. All other affects are related to these basic three. Joy (*laetitia*), for Spinoza, is "that passion by which the mind passes to a greater perfection."[3] The first feature that distinguishes joy from the other affects is that it indicates the move from a lesser to a greater perfection. The immediate difficulty with this conception of joy is the meaning of "perfection" here. What is perfection and how does joy move one from lesser to greater perfection? Perfection does not here indicate flawlessness, but completion. For Spinoza humans are always a work in progress, and they express degrees of completeness or perfection. If we think of a house in the process of being built, for example, it is easy to imagine triumphs and setbacks in this process. The distinction between a triumph and setback is also easy to determine. Triumphs are those events that lead toward the completion of the house, a solid foundation, a squared frame, good plumbing, etc. Spinoza calls those ways of affecting and being affected that lead us closer to completion "joys."

By the same token, setbacks are those events that lead away from the completion of the house. Numerous types of setbacks are possible. One could imagine a storm that damages the frame. One could imagine plumbing that fails inspection and would thus need to be replaced. One could even imagine a flawed plan whereby different components of the house are destructive to one another, for example, a cantilevered addition that actually forces the remainder of the house off the foundation. Ways of affecting and being affected that lead away from completion, Spinoza calls "sadness," (*tristitia*) and its definition mirrors joy in all but one respect, "that passion by which it [mind] passes to a lesser perfection."[4]

The other feature that distinguishes joy and sadness from the other affects is that both are passions. We discussed Spinoza's use of "passion" briefly above. "Passions" indicate those ways of affecting and being affected in which we are passive. So, on the one hand, joy and sadness are opposed insofar as joy indicates greater perfection while sadness indicates lesser perfection. On the other hand, both are similar in that both are passions. Or, to combine this with Spinoza's understanding of adequate and inadequate causes, joy and sadness are affects of which we are the inadequate cause. Joy and sadness are something that happens to us, rather than ways that we *act*.

In order to illustrate this further, let's look at a few examples of affects based on joy and sadness. "Hate is nothing but sadness with the accompanying idea of an external cause."[5] Admittedly, this seems like a strange way to talk about hate, but let's start with what we know already: Hate is a kind of sadness. What Spinoza means by this is that hate is a way of being affected that leads away from completion. To this Spinoza adds the additional condition that this damaging way of being affected is accompanied by the idea of an external cause. As I made clear at the outset, I have a dislike for SUVs bordering on the psychotic. Do I really hate SUVs, though? Part of my hesitance lies in my upbringing. I was taught never to say "hate," especially in reference to people. As a result, I'm always engaging in euphemisms and circumlocutions to avoid saying it. The fact of the matter is, though, that SUVs are always in my way. On a grand scale, they use too much gas. On a more particular scale, they impede vision. They take up too much room in parking lots and on the road. SUVs are a continual source of distress whether they're actually present, or I'm just thinking about them. In either case I become distracted. I'm no longer capable of acting the way I was before the SUV came up. So, in the case of my road rage, whatever I was thinking about or doing suddenly becomes derailed by the revenge fantasy I now seem obligated to spin. This seems like a clear instance of moving from greater perfection to lesser perfection (and thus a kind of sadness), which has its source in an external cause, the SUV (and thus hate). This is made even clearer by the discussion that follows Spinoza's definition of hate. "[O]ne who hates strives to remove and destroy the thing he hates."[6] My revenge fantasy clearly involves the disabling of one SUV, but undoubtedly lying behind it is the dream of omnipotence where I could remove all SUVs at will. For Spinoza this is a clear-cut case of hate, but as we saw above the goal is not to give into my hate, but understand the world in such a way that my hate becomes impossible.

Love in contrast to hate (but not complete contrast) is "joy with the accompanying idea of an external cause."[7] Structurally, the definitions are identical. The difference between love and hate lies in the fact that some of the ways that we are affected lead us away from completion as does hate. Other affects, though, lead us toward completion. These are the joyful affects, and love is a principal example. At this point a tension arises between the romantic conception of love as highest, greatest, most world-conquering state that one could ever into, and the rather mundane way we actually use the word. It's true that we use the word "love" to refer to a uniquely human and transcendent emotional state, but we use the exact same word to talk about shoes, food, and TV shows. Can this tension be reconciled? Or, should we reserve "love" for the higher state and "like" for everyday use? Perhaps, we could invent new words as Woody Allen's character Alvy Singer suggests in *Annie Hall*: "lōve," "lurve," or "luff (with two f's)." None of these are particularly satisfying for Spinoza who opts to give an account of "love" as we actually use it from the ridiculous to the sublime. Love is nothing but those ways of being affected by external causes that lead toward our completion. Here we see the impetus that leads us to distinguish between types of love to the point that we want to claim there is a difference in quality. For Spinoza, there is clearly a difference among all the different uses of "love," but that difference lies in the external cause. Some external causes only lead me a little way toward completion, a good meal, for example. Insofar as that's the case, though, I unproblematically say, "I loved that meal." There are other external causes that are a great deal more helpful in moving me toward completion, family, friends, and education. All of these I love, and all of these I love differently. Why do I love them differently? Because, as different external causes they all affect me in different ways but nonetheless move me toward completion. If we return to the scene from *The Simpsons* with which we began the chapter, we can see that Dr. Hibbert was asking exactly the right question. What kind of love is being brought here? How are you proposing to affect me? In what way are you going to bring me closer to completion?

So far in our discussion of Spinoza's theory of the affects we have been using the notion of "completion" or "perfection" without much precision. In the same way that Aristotle mused that one could easily define a good harp player or a good ditch digger, but that defining a good person was a more complicated matter, so, it is easy for us to identify a completed house or a completed action, but not so easy define what it would mean to be a complete person. In order to answer this question, Spinoza proposes the third of his three basic affects, striving (*conatus*). "Each thing, as far as it can by its own power, *strives* to persevere in its being."[8] Notice that Spinoza does not restrict striving to humans. *Everything* strives to persevere. I take Spinoza literally here. Not only do people strive to persevere, but so do plants, rocks, and telephones. In what sense, though, can we say that phones strive to persevere? The phone has no will. It doesn't want anything. Isn't Spinoza guilty of an egregious anthropomorphism? Spinoza would say that certainly the phone doesn't have a will or want anything, but it does continue existing unless something external to it destroys it. The phone will even resist destruction (which is the same as persevering) to the degree that it is able. Again, the phone's power to resist destruction is not a result of conscious activity, but merely a function of its construction. Because the phone is made of hard plastic and not, say, cream cheese, it is able to resist destruction or persevere more readily.

What something is and its ability to persevere are, then, one and the same. Spinoza says it this way, "[t]he striving by which each thing strives to persevere in its being is nothing but the actual essence of the thing."[9] Here Spinoza explicitly connects "striving" and "essence." The straightforward claim here is that striving makes a thing what it is. Or, in the traditional language of necessary conditions (*sine qua non*), without striving nothing can be itself. At the same time that Spinoza appropriates the traditional vocabulary of philosophy, he is also breaking with it in an important way. Since at least Aristotle, the essence of a thing has two aspects. First, the essence is a property of the thing. Thus for Aristotle, the essence of humans is reason. Second, and this is related to the first, the essence must be the property that distinguishes one class of things from another. Humans are defined by reason precisely because reason is what humans possess that no other thing possesses. Humans are identified by their specific difference. Hence, Aristotle's definition of humans is taken up in the medieval tradition as "rational animal." In contrast to this, Spinoza is claiming that striving defines, is the essence of, all things. This immediately flies in the face of the traditional distinctions of philosophy that sharply distinguish the human and the animal, and the animate and inanimate. Striving is the essence of all of these. Where then, does the distinction lie? Spinoza cannot be claiming that there is no difference among amoebas, lawnmowers, and humans. The difference lies in the striving itself. Amoebas strive differently from both lawnmowers and humans, and each of these strive differently from each other and amoebas. Quite simply, striving refers to the ways that a thing can affect other things. For an amoeba, this striving amounts to very little most of the time. An amoeba perseveres in existence by controlling the comings and goings of other single-celled organisms around it. A little bleach in the water can really ruin its day. On the other hand, if ingested by a human the amoeba can wreak great havoc merely by persevering in existence. Given the differences in their ways of striving, though, an amoeba has no effect on a lawnmower. Steel and plastic lie beyond its striving. As we'll see below, understanding things in terms of their ways of affecting and being affected provides an important corrective to dominant ways of thinking in the Western tradition.

What concerns us here, however, is an overview of Spinoza's theory of the affects. As we have seen, two of the basic affects, joy and sadness, are passions. That is, both refer to ways that we are acted upon by external causes. In contrast to this, striving is not a passion but an action. Striving indicates the ways in which we act in accordance with our nature. It is here that we are able to answer the question that arose above in regard to completion or perfection. We are complete to the degree that we act, or we are complete to the degree that we are the adequate cause of our affects rather than the inadequate cause of our affects. Thus, for Spinoza there are two basic types of affects that indicate our activity, or "strength of character" (*for-titudo*): "tenacity" (*animositas*) and "nobility" (*generositas*).

> Those actions, therefore, which aim only at the agent's advantage, I relate to tenacity, and those which aim at another's advantage, I relate to nobility. So moderation, sobriety, presence of mind in danger, etc., are species of tenacity whereas courtesy, mercy, etc., are species of nobility.[10]

In the chapters that follow we will continue to explore the wide-ranging implications of Spinoza's theory of the affects. For right now, however, let's return to getting cut off by the SUV driver. As we've already seen, I was affected negatively by this event. I was diminished rather than strengthened, made less complete. Why? Because at that point, I was not the adequate cause of my actions. My actions could not be explained through me alone, but only through the way I was being affected by the external cause of the SUV. Some might argue, though, that I was watching out for myself. By asserting myself, however impotently, I was being tenacious. A little reflection, however, shows that this is not the case. Does road rage tend to lead toward or away from my perseverance? Am I more or less likely to get into an accident in this state, or when I'm prudent and keep my wits about me? For Spinoza, road rage would not be a case of tenacity, where I strive toward perseverance. This is borne out by the conclusion of the event. Only when I finally understand why I was cut off do I become active rather than passive. Only then can I seek not only my advantage (tenacity) but the advantage of others (nobility).

NOTES

1. IA1.
2. Eventually, we'll see that adequacy lies on a continuum for Spinoza. The path of wisdom lies in the direction of being an adequate cause, although we can never eliminate our dependence on external causes.
3. IIIP11S.
4. IIIP11S. We'll return to Spinoza's conception of perfection when we discuss Spinoza's conception of God in chapter 9, but for right now the relevant analogue is grammar. The perfect tense indicates an action that is already completed. If I say, "I've been hit by an SUV," it means that at some point prior to now the action of being hit by an SUV has been completed.
5. IIIP13S.
6. IIIP13S.
7. IIIP13S.
8. IIIP6.
9. IIIP7.
10. IIIP59S.

Chapter 3
On Not Being Oneself,
Or the Shmoopy Effect

In the *Seinfeld* episode, "The Soup Nazi," Jerry has a new girlfriend. Inexplicably they call each other "shmoopy." They have long conversations with one another about who is in fact shmoopy. George and Elaine find this insufferable. George goes on the counteroffensive by mirroring Jerry's behavior when he's with his fiancée, Susan. This creates an escalating war of public affection as both couples end up making out in the coffee shop. Ultimately, balance is restored late in the episode when Jerry breaks up with his new girlfriend.

The question that concerns me here is Jerry's behavior and George's reaction to it. Both George and Jerry have a continual series of girlfriends throughout the show, and while it is sometimes the source of tension, usually George and Jerry work together to solve the tension (most famously in "The Switch" where Jerry tries to date the roommate of the woman he is currently dating). In the shmoopy incident, though, George's primary response is to avoid Jerry as much as possible. Why? Clearly he finds Jerry's behavior irritating, but this simply begs the question. George's problem is that Jerry is not acting like himself when he's around the new girlfriend.

I take it we've all had the experience of being around someone not acting like him or herself. The classic example is a college roommate who begins the semester as a good friend with thoughtful, predictable behavior, but once he begins dating, morphs into a completely different person. On further reflection, however, this is a really strange expression. How is it possible for one not to act like oneself? If I'm acting, then am I not necessarily acting like myself? When I'm not acting like myself, am I acting like someone else? This seems less likely. It's not as if Jerry is acting like his girlfriend. George never claims that Jerry is acting like his girlfriend or anyone else for that matter. The problem is, he's not himself.

It seems that the possibility that one can on occasion not coincide with oneself reveals some tacit assumptions that we have about the self. The first assumption is that there is a constancy to the self. The self, who a person is, somehow persists through time. This persisting self has two aspects. Some of the qualities that define who we are given genetically, qualities like height, shoe size, or lactose intolerance. Other qualities are acquired throughout life. Many of these qualities are acquired unconsciously, hand gestures, verbal tics, posture, etc. These unconsciously acquired properties are naturally susceptible to conscious manipulation, but for the most part their acquisition and deployment remain unconscious. Finally, there are qualities that define us that we acquire only consciously. Learning to play an instrument or a sport would fall into this category, and for most moral philosophers so would being a good person. The self is thus this complex nexus of given and acquired traits that remain relatively stable.

Philosophers have traditionally made a distinction between these two kinds of traits in terms of nature. Given traits are referred to as "nature," while acquired traits are referred to as "second nature." We still use this distinction today in claims like, "Playing basketball is second nature to her." The force of the claim is that she plays basketball as if she were genetically programmed to do so. However, her playing basketball is actually the result of years of practice acquiring the traits of a good basketball player. The acquisition of traits is usually referred to as habit. Aristotle helpfully distinguishes among three stages in the acquisition of habit. The first stage is the capacity to form the habit. Humans, for example, do not have the capacity to fly under their own power. Thus, no matter how hard they try, they cannot develop the habit of flying. Humans do, however, have the capacity to play basketball. The game was designed specifically with humans in mind. Having the capacity to play basketball and playing basketball are very different things. Just because it is not opposed to my nature to play basketball does not mean that the first time I walk onto a court I will know what to do.

What is missing from my capacity to play basketball is instruction and practice. I need to learn the rules of the game. I need to learn how much force is required to shoot a free throw and differentiate that from shooting a three-point shot. I must actually develop my capacities in order to form a habit. On the way to forming a habit, though, I will invariably do a few things right purely by accident. It's conceivable that upon walking on the court for the first time, I pick up a basketball and sink a half-court shot. Everyone might cheer, but no one would confuse me for a good basketball player. Exercising a capacity prior to forming a habit is the second stage of habit formation. Habits cannot form without practice, but the practice is not necessarily, especially initially, habitual. It is only when I consistently make half-court shots that I have developed the habit and might be considered a good basketball player. It is only when playing basketball has become second nature to me—when I have developed all of the appropriate habits—that my habit formation is complete. This last step is the most difficult to achieve of Aristotle's three stages.

The principal aspect of habit that separates it from its acquisition is its permanency. If I continually practice and after much hard work possess the habits of a good basketball player, these habits remain remarkably engrained. For example, when I played football in middle and high school, one of the habits engrained in us was to yell, "Ball!" if there was a fumble. We were required to yell it whether we were in the play or on the sidelines. To this day, some twenty-five years later, I cannot watch football at any level, whether live or on TV, without yelling, "Ball!" when I see a fumble. While my wife finds this somewhat amusing, it is also another indication for her of my none-too-firm grasp on reality.

This short detour through habit and its acquisition leads us back to the presuppositions that we have about the self. As we've seen, because of habit there is a certain stability to the self. Otherwise, the claim that one is not oneself would be meaningless. However, the second tacit assumption that makes such a claim possible is that the self is *not* absolutely stable. One necessarily develops habits that cover a huge range of activities, but these are not so set that one cannot on occasion act against them. What makes Jerry's behavior so vexing to George is that neither is particularly affectionate. In fact, one could argue that *Seinfeld* is predicated on all of the characters' complete lack of sentiment. George and Jerry's disdain for affection, particularly public affection, is highlighted in "The Kiss Hello." In this episode Jerry continually finds himself in situations where he's required to kiss as a form of greeting. He finds this intolerable and expresses real admiration for George who is only required to kiss his Aunt Sylvia hello. The lengths to which Jerry goes to opt out of the kiss hello leave him ostracized from all of the other tenants in his apartment building. George is understandably appalled when the same Jerry who would rather be an outcast than kiss someone hello is kissing and snuggling in public while calling and being called "shmoopy."

Jerry has clearly developed the habit of not displaying affection publicly. That's who he is. He is able, however briefly, to set aside this habit and act differently to the extent that George no longer recognizes him. How is this possible? Habits are overcome in the same way that they are formed, through practice. For example, everyone has a habitual way in which he or she interlaces fingers and thumbs. For right-handed people this is generally with the left thumb on top. Regardless of how it is done, one way will feel comfortable ("natural"), and the other way will feel uncomfortable ("unnatural"). Remarkably, it is possible to reverse these feelings and make it so that having the opposite thumb on top feels "natural." This, of course, is only possible because what is at stake here is not "nature" in the traditional sense but "second nature." We can change our habits not by fiat or force of will but by practicing something opposed until a new habit forms. Thus, if I continually practice interlacing my fingers the other way with the opposite thumb on top, eventually this will become my habit. This will become comfortable, second nature. Habits are instilled through practice and replaced by practicing something in opposition to the original habit. What happened in the case of Jerry's new girlfriend is that he began practicing actions that were opposed to his previous habits. When he did this he was no longer what George expected, and George found this insufferable. Fortunately, however, the new practices he was engaged in did not replace his old habit, and by the end of the episode he is the same old Jerry.

Spinoza is very interested in those points when we are not ourselves and he devotes the fourth part of the *Ethics* to giving an account of this phenomenon. To this end Spinoza writes, "There is no singular thing in nature than which there is not another more powerful and stronger."[1] Spinoza takes it as axiomatic that no matter how big or strong something is, there is always something stronger out there. This seems like a strange way to begin talking about why someone is not behaving in a typical manner. But, recall that Spinoza's primary concern is the difference between the path of wisdom and the path of foolishness, and the difference between these two paths lies in the numerous ways that we might affect and be affected by the things around us. In this light Spinoza's claim is that it is possible to be affected in such a way that we are overpowered by what affects us. No matter how powerful we are, it is always possible to be overpowered. When we are not ourselves, it means we have overcome by something more powerful.

The question of power and being overpowered returns us to the definitions of adequate and inadequate cause. When we are the adequate cause of an effect, when we act, it can only mean that we are not at that moment being overpowered by some other cause. To be overpowered by another cause is the same as being an inadequate cause. In the example from the previous chapter where I'm struck by an SUV while crossing the street, this is a clear instance of when I'm being overpowered, passive.

Adequate and inadequate causes, of course, return us to the affects. Some of the effects are passions, those following from joy and sadness, and some of the affects are actions, those following from striving. From this perspective we can see that one is not oneself when one is overcome by those affects that are passions. Jerry is not himself with his new girlfriend, because he is overcome by the passion that Spinoza calls "love." That is, Jerry is moving from a state of lesser perfection to greater perfection, but the source of this movement is the external cause of the new girlfriend.

As we saw above in Spinoza's axiom we are always "bumping" into things that are more powerful than we are. When we do our direction will necessarily change. If I'm walking down the hall and run into a door frame, I do not continue in the same direction at the same speed and plow through the wall. Rather, I'm stopped dead in my tracks or spun sideways while I try and regain my balance. While it's easy to illustrate the principle at work here physically, Spinoza has a much broader application in mind. There are innumerable ways that I can be affected by the world around me. It's tempting to think of power in terms of size, but power for Spinoza is very specific and means "can have an effect." So, while I'm obviously affected by running into an immovable object like a door frame, or by a much larger object running into me like an SUV, there are also very small objects that can have an effect on me like a virus or an amoeba. Whenever I encounter something like this that affects me, takes me away from my usual habits and into different practices, I am not myself. In this respect, it's not uncommon for someone recovering from an illness to say, "I'm beginning to feel like myself again." In addition to the possibility that we might be affected by both large and small physical objects, we can also be affected by things that we might not consider physical, like love or hate. While the source of love or hate is certainly an external cause, this seems different from a collision with a physical object or an infection. But, Spinoza boils all of these encounters down to their basic structure. We're always bumping into things, walls, germs, other people, etc. Sometimes these encounters change our direction. The change in direction might be subtle and momentary. Nobody would claim that we are not ourselves after running into a wall. However, an illness might certainly engender this claim as well as a new boyfriend or girlfriend.

The great danger, as far as Spinoza is concerned, is that the change engendered might radically alter our practices and become new habits, permanently changing who we are. Spinoza writes, "The force of any passion, or affect, can surpass the other actions, or power, of a man, so that the affect stubbornly clings to the man."[2] Fortunately for Jerry this did not happen in his case. His actions were changed briefly, but they didn't "stubbornly cling" to him. The clearest example of what Spinoza is speaking about lies in addiction. If we take alcoholism, for example, we see a case where a person changes under the power of the external cause. The person becomes dependent on the change wrought by alcohol, and the behaviors associated with its consumption become habitual. The alcoholic is a different person when drinking. His acts are no longer his own. He is no longer the adequate cause of his actions, but the inadequate cause. Or, in order to explain why an alcoholic is such, we cannot explain them from his nature alone. His actions can only be explained by the combination of the alcoholic and the alcohol.

This problem of not being oneself, Spinoza calls "bondage" (*servitus*). Anytime we are overcome by causes opposed to our nature, we are in bondage. That is, our actions can only be explained by the combination of us and some external cause. The tempting solution to the problem of bondage is simply to remove ourselves from the influence of external causes. For Spinoza, this is simply not possible. While we will explore this more fully in later chapters, removing oneself from the influence of external causes is tantamount to removing oneself from the world. Remember, Spinoza takes it as axiomatic that we are always bumping into things and that sometimes what we bump into will overpower us.

At this point it seems that we are doomed to bondage. If we necessarily bump into things, and some of those things will overpower us, how can we ever escape bondage? Another way that this question might be posed is, are all changes bad? Isn't it possible that the change wrought in me by acquiring a new habit would be helpful rather than harmful, a step down the path of wisdom rather than foolishness? Is saying that "one is not oneself" necessarily pejorative? Can't one be better than one used to be? While we will answer these questions more fully in the following chapters, Spinoza is quite clear that bondage is not the only fate that awaits us. It is possible to act rather than be acted upon. It is possible to affect rather than be affected. There is a path of wisdom in addition to a path of foolishness. The path of wisdom lies beyond both sadness and joy in what Spinoza calls "freedom."

While saving our discussion of freedom for a later chapter, it is possible to think about the way in which some changes can be good. First, for Spinoza since we cannot remove ourselves from the world and are in a constant state of affecting and being affected, the answer must lie in the affects themselves. Thus the goal of Spinoza's practical philosophy is not Stoic indifference or lack of affect but a fruitful engagement with the affects. In this regard Spinoza writes, "An affect cannot be restrained or taken away except by an affect opposite to, and stronger than, the affect to be restrained."[3] Affectlessness is not an option. The only possibility is replacing one affect with another stronger one. For the most part this is an unconscious process. We go through the day experiencing a range of emotions, each one replacing the one before it. So, if we imagine that I am particularly sad one day, I will remain in that sadness until another stronger emotion comes to take its place. It's entirely possible that a funny YouTube video might snap me out of my funk, a clip from the Daily Show or a monkey riding a dog. However, it's also possible that while my sadness might be briefly overcome, in the end the new affect was not strong enough to take hold, and I remain in my sadness. Regardless of what happens, though, the path to change, whether good or bad, happens through the affects rather than in spite of them.

> Again, . . . it follows that we can never bring it about that we require nothing outside ourselves to preserve our being, nor that we live without having dealings with things outside us. . . . There are, therefore, many things outside us which are useful to us, and on that account to be sought.[4]

One of the primary ways that we affect or are affected by external causes is through food. We must eat to live and so sating our hunger is part of our striving. Going from hungry to full is the movement from lesser to greater perfection. (Although, eating beyond fullness moves us from greater to lesser perfection.) Not everything that we eat, though, is of equal value. Some foods are better for us than others, and some foods are downright detrimental to our health. When I consume nourishing foods, the change that's produced in me is a positive one. If, however, I consume unhealthy food, the change produced in me is negative. In the first case, I strengthen who I am by combining with things that agree with my nature. In the second case, I weaken who I am by combining with things opposed to my nature. It is in this instance that we can see more fully what is meant by the phrase that a certain food "doesn't agree with me." On the surface, the claim is that a food is the source of some intestinal distress. The real issue, though, is that something opposed to one's nature has been ingested, and what one strove for out of hunger resulted in being affected negatively. Aversion to foods that sicken us is one of the few habits that can be developed almost instantaneously. Spinoza would say to the degree that one is "thrown off course" by disagreeable food, one is in bondage. Furthermore, to the degree that what one eats is agreeable (not only in the short term but the long term), one is not in bondage.

In "The Soup Nazi" Jerry is in bondage to his new girlfriend. She is an external cause that throws him off course and makes him obnoxious to his friends. In the end, Jerry breaks up with her and his explanation is quite interesting. George's fiancée, Susan, mentions to Jerry that he really likes his new girlfriend, and Jerry responds by saying that, while they had great affection for one another, "mentally, we couldn't quite make the connection." Jerry realizes that, while his girlfriend was undoubtedly the source of joy, ultimately they weren't enough alike to make a lasting relationship. The new girlfriend was like delicious but unhealthy food. Candy tastes great and agrees with us in some respects, but a steady diet of it would be profoundly detrimental. What was lacking, as far as Jerry was concerned, was an intellectual connection. In this vein Spinoza writes, "For if, for example, two individuals of entirely the same nature are joined to one another, they compose an individual twice as powerful as each one."[5] Jerry realized that by joining with someone who did not agree with him both physically and mentally, he was diminishing his ability to affect the world. The combination with the new girlfriend weakened him by leaving him open to external causes that he wouldn't ordinarily be affected by. This is why Jerry wasn't himself. This is the shmoopy effect. This is bondage.

Looking back at the case of road rage from the first chapter, we can see things a little more clearly. First, it's clear that one of the habits that defined me at the time was an extreme reaction to the ways I was being affected while driving. Driving almost always resulted in affects related to sadness rather than joy or striving. In particular, hatred and anger were the most common affects. My sadness was dependent on the other drivers as an external cause. Furthermore, my hatred drove me to do evil to the object of my hatred. Fortunately for me, my evil acts remained at the level of fantasy, so that I'm writing this book rather than sitting in jail. Nevertheless my road rage was an occasion where I was ruled by my passions. Or, what is the same thing for Spinoza, I was the inadequate cause rather than the adequate cause of my actions. The amazing thing here is that these actions are mostly localized in my own head. A person driving ten yards or so ahead of me with no knowledge of my existence has somehow managed to seize control of my thoughts, words, and gestures. If this seems like an extreme appraisal of the situation, consider the possibility that I'm not cut off. Do I still swear and gesticulate wildly? Do I still construct elaborate revenge fantasies? This seems wholly unlikely. The more plausible answer is that my actions cannot be explained from me alone. My actions can only be explained by my encounter, my being affected by an external cause. If I am being controlled by something other than myself and that is in fact detrimental to me, how can this be understood as anything other than bondage?

For Spinoza the primary ethical problem to be solved is the problem of human bondage. How is it possible, given that we are constantly being affected by external causes, to ever be ourselves? Given the kind of world we live in, how can we act? How can we ever be the adequate cause of our actions? The answer clearly lies in replacing affects that are passions with affects that are active. This is the only avenue open to us, since being unaffected is not an option for Spinoza. But, how do we replace one affect with another? For the most part it seems that the changing from one affect to another is unconscious. Furthermore, what would it mean to have an active affect? What exactly do tenacity and nobility look like in practice? We have already seen the contours of Spinoza's answer to these questions in the case of road rage from chapter 1. As we saw, my anger continued to spin out of control until I understood *why* I was cut off. Once I saw the SUV stop at the hospital and a pregnant woman being helped out of the passenger's side, my anger dissipated and was replaced by other affects: surprise, relief, guilt, etc., to the degree that I understood I was no longer angry. Understanding, then, must be the key for Spinoza. Understanding must be a way in which we become the adequate rather than the inadequate cause of our actions. Before we explore what the understanding is and how it leads away from bondage, however, we need to know a little bit more about who we are and where we are. For Spinoza, we cannot know how the human understanding works without first coming to grips with the mind, and we cannot come to grips with the mind without understanding where we fit in the big scheme of things, that is, our place in the universe.

NOTES

1. IVA1.
2. IVP6.
3. IVP7.
4. IVP18S.
5. IVP18S.

Chapter 4
The Big Picture

In order to fully grasp how understanding might help us in overcoming bondage to external causes, we need to prepare for some conceptual heavy lifting and take a step back and look at the big picture. In fact, we need to look at the biggest picture imaginable, the picture that contains all other pictures. Already this lands us in some conceptual difficulties. Is such a picture possible? Is such a picture thinkable? It is precisely the claim that there was in fact a big picture that contained all other pictures that got Spinoza in so much trouble—a trouble that not only pursued him while he was alive, requiring him to publish some of his books anonymously and even posthumously in the case of the *Ethics*, but sullied his reputation after his death. Many would say that the problem with the one big picture model is that it's a kind of monism, meaning that everything is one. While this might initially seem fairly benign, the fact of the matter is that it doesn't seem to leave any room for a traditional conception of God. On this reading, Spinoza doesn't have a theism, which requires a necessary and insuperable gap between God and the rest of the universe. He has a pantheism, which makes God part of the universe, or more precisely makes God identical with the universe. For many during Spinoza's time and even today, this is tantamount to atheism. We'll look at the religious implications of Spinoza's thought in a later chapter. What I want to do now, though, is look at why Spinoza thought there was only one big picture.

Let's begin with the axiom that we used as an example in chapter 2: "Whatever is, is either in itself or in another."[1] For Spinoza it is self-evident that everything can be exhaustively accounted for in terms of that which contains and that which is contained. Let's see where this distinction leads us. If I think about the chair I'm currently sitting in and ask whether it contains or is contained, it appears to be contained. The container that holds my chair is my office, but my office really isn't a container either, because my office is contained in my building. Furthermore, my building is contained by my campus, which is contained by the town where the college is. The town is contained by the county and the county the state. The state is of course contained by the country, which is contained by the continent, which is contained by the hemisphere. All of which is contained by the earth. The earth, while a very big picture, is not the biggest picture. The earth is part of the solar system, which is part of a galaxy. The galaxy is part of a galaxy cluster, and this cluster is part of the universe as a whole.

The universe, however, seems to be the point where this gradually increasing vista stops. Everything else seems to be contained within the universe, but the universe does not seem to be contained by anything else. To illustrate this, let's try a thought experiment. Suppose we try to imagine something outside of the universe, say, an extra-dimensional universe that lies parallel to our own. It seems that two options are possible for conceiving of this additional universe. Either it lies utterly beyond our comprehension and cannot have any contact with our universe, or we imagine it as lying alongside our universe either spatially or temporally. In the first case, it is meaningless to talk about such a universe. Such a parallel universe could only be conceived as related to our universe in some way, which brings us to the second possibility. In the case of the second possibility, though, notice what happens. Even though we speak of two "universes," what is actually the case is that we're forced to conceive of a greater whole that contains both our universe and the alternate universe. But, isn't this greater whole, this bigger picture really what we mean by "universe"? "Universe" is simply the word we use to refer to the biggest possible picture, the picture that contains all that there is. In Spinoza's terms the universe is the only thing that is "in itself," while everything else is "in another." The other that everything else is in is the whole, the totality, the universe, nature, and here Spinoza introduces two new terms for what is in itself: "substance" and "God." The first term is relatively unproblematic. By appropriating "substance" Spinoza places himself in a long philosophical tradition that stretches all the way back to Aristotle and culminates in Descartes, Spinoza's immediate precursor. The use of "God," as simply another name for the universe or nature, landed Spinoza in all kinds of hot water, as we saw above.

For now, though, let's stick with substance to see what that tells us about the big picture. While Spinoza is clearly attempting to criticize the traditional conception of substance, it is Descartes that is his immediate target. Descartes famously said, "I think, therefore, I am," and argues on the basis of this statement that there must be two substances. On the one hand, the fact that I think necessarily entails that I exist. It would be impossible to think and not exist. As for existing and not thinking, Descartes would say that it's possible, but such a state would not be knowable as when we sleep without dreaming. What follows from this for Descartes is that humans are essentially thinking things. A mind without a body is conceivable. We can imagine that our identity remains intact even without a body. On the other hand, we would not identify with a mindless body. If we imagine a mindless body the first thing that probably comes to mind is a corpse. For Descartes we are our mind, and although body and mind are related, we are not our bodies. This raises the question, though, about the nature of bodies. Even if we accept that our essence is mental, what status does the body have? Descartes takes it as obvious that bodies are fundamentally different from minds. The properties of each seem completely opposed. Bodies are spatial; minds are not. Bodies are divisible; minds are not. And most importantly for Descartes, bodies are mortal; minds are immortal. The only way that Descartes can account for these opposed properties is by locating them in different substances. Traditionally, a substance is simply that in which properties or attributes inhere. As a result, a substance cannot contain contradictory properties. Such a substance would destroy itself. Thus for Descartes, there must be two substances, one that contains the properties of thought and one that contains the properties of bodies or extended things.

The problem that immediately arises for Descartes, and his critics were keen to point this out, is if mind and body belong to different substances precisely because they share no common properties, how can mind and body communicate? How can the spatial communicate with the non-spatial? How can the visible communicate with the invisible? How can the mortal communicate with the immortal? The problem is precisely the problem of mediation. We are required to imagine something that shares the property of both mind and body as a go-between. Descartes infamously imagined that in the blood flowed tiny particles called "animal spirits" that would agitate the pineal gland in order to communicate the sensations of the body to the mind. Or, conversely, the mind would agitate the pineal gland in order to transmit its commands to the animal spirits, which would then carry them to the appropriate part of the body. But, how precisely does this happen? Blood particles and pineal glands are material. Furthermore, vibrations are also material. How can material vibrations in space be conveyed to the non-material, non-spatial mind? Additionally, how can the immaterial mind agitate the pineal gland? It can't use force, which is material. Nor can it send vibrations, which are also material. Descartes has so clearly and thoroughly separated mind and body, that he cannot get them back together again.

The source of Descartes' difficulties, as far as Spinoza is concerned, is his positing of two substances. Substances cannot have anything in common with one another, even on Descartes' understanding. Otherwise, the substances are not "in themselves." For Spinoza, there must be a bigger picture that contains both mind and body. This is, of course, the universe as a whole, which contains both thoughts (with all the characteristics described by Descartes) and extended things (with all the properties unique to bodies). This immediately solves the communication problem. The reason that mind and body can communicate is that both belong to the same substance.

We'll explore the relation between mind and body more fully in the next chapter, but for now let's look at another component of Spinoza's big picture that's related directly to the relation between mind and body. In one respect Spinoza solves the problem created by Descartes' substance dualism by denying it and positing a substance monism in its place. This doesn't entirely solve the problem, though. Spinoza would agree with Descartes that minds and bodies do have opposed properties, so how can they coexist in the same substance? It's at this point that Spinoza introduces the notion of "attribute" in order to more fully flesh out his big picture. "By attribute I understand what the intellect perceives of a substance, as constituting its essence."[2] Attributes are thus ways of looking at substance, stories one might tell about the big picture. One might say that the scientific discipline of physics is precisely this kind of big picture story. Physics assumes that the universe is physical and seeks to give an account of it purely within those terms. The reason that physics is a fruitful, progressive science is that it sees the world for what it essentially (but not wholly) is, a system of physical interactions. By the same token, it's also possible to tell a big picture story from the perspective of human emotion and willing, as a novelist might do. The reason some novels "ring true" is that they also see the world for what it essentially (but not wholly) is, a series of emotional connections between people and the world. These two types of stories are not exclusive of one another. Both may be told because both see the world for what it essentially is. The big picture contains both minds and bodies, and a true account may be given from either perspective. Furthermore, there is no conflict between these two accounts any more than there is conflict between a novel and physics. They are simply different orders of discourse about different attributes of the same thing.

The last piece to Spinoza's big picture is all of the little pieces that make up the big picture. These he calls "modes." As Spinoza writes, "By mode I understand the affections of a substance, *or* that which is in another through which it is also conceived."[3] Modes are simply the parts of the whole. Immediately, we see the breadth of Spinoza's notion of affect. It's not just humans that affect and are affected. The whole universe can be thought of as a system of affections. Everything that happens, no matter how large or how small, is an affect of the universe. Or, if we ask "where" something happens, whether it's two atoms colliding, me walking to the coffee shop, or a star going supernova, it is always correct to say, "in the universe." The big picture is logically prior to all the little parts that make it up. For Spinoza, it is impossible to imagine the part without first assuming the whole. Notice, though, this is logical priority, not temporal priority. It's not that there was once an empty, undifferentiated universe waiting to be filled, and then it was filled at a later time. No, in the same way that my hand presupposes me, even though I've always been coexistent with my hand, any part of the universe presupposes the universe as a whole. Substance always precedes its modifications. If there were no whole, one could not think of the parts as parts. Or, we need the whole to think of the parts as parts.

We'll look more closely at modes in later chapters. For now suffice it to say that any change in the universe is the result of modes (or parts of the whole) affecting one another, and that the notion of "part" depends on the scale of one's perspective. Thus, we can speak about subatomic particles interacting with one another, people interacting with one another, or galaxies colliding with one another. Regardless of the scale though, these interactions among the parts are always thought on the basis of the whole. That is, they are all part of something larger than themselves.

Now that we have the major components of Spinoza's big picture in place, his metaphysics or ontology, we can get a better idea of how the universe works. The first claim that follows from the definition of substance for Spinoza is that it's infinite. However, Spinoza is not using "infinite" in the way that we normally think about it. Analogous to his use of "perfect" above, "infinite" does not mean "unending"; this is the mathematical conception of infinity, the idea that whatever number we think of, we can always add one more. This meaning of "infinite" is certainly contained in the etymology of the word. Another meaning is possible, though, and this becomes clear if we think about "infinite" as "unlimited." Obviously, the mathematical determination comes to the fore, but "unlimited" can also mean "not limited by anything else." What it would be to be limited by something else is to be defined in relation to it. Thus, the definition of any object contains both its positive properties (what it is) and its negative properties (what it is not). Or, as Aristotle would say the definition of something lies in its specific difference. We first discover what large group an object belongs to (genus). In the case of humans, for Aristotle, we are animals. This is not definitive, since we are not merely animals. What differentiates us from animals is our reason. This is our specific difference (species). We are defined only by our relation to something else, how we are both similar to and different from animals. Anything that must be defined in its relations to others is thus "finite," limited precisely by the fact that it's related. The opposite of this, of course, is "infinite" not limited precisely because it's unrelated to anything else. The only thing that fits this bill for Spinoza is substance, the universe, the big picture. Nothing about this understanding of "infinite," however, entails that the universe is infinite in the mathematical sense. The only thing that follows is that the universe must contain all that is. If it does not, then something lies outside of the universe to limit it, and we must redraw a big picture to contain both what we thought was the "universe" and what lies beyond it. Only the new picture will be properly called "the universe."

The next thing we need to know about Spinoza's universe is that there are two fundamental perspectives from which one might view it. One may view from the perspective of the parts or from the perspective of the whole. This distinction is codified for us in terms of a forest and its trees. It is possible to "miss the forest for the trees." The implication, of course is that one fails to see the big picture, because one is too caught up in the parts. The obverse is also possible, but more rarely invoked. One may "miss the trees for the forest," that is, see things so broadly and from such a distance that the parts become an undifferentiated mass. Although, Spinoza is sometimes accused of advocating the former at the expense of the latter, he would say parts and whole work together in tandem, and understanding involves knowledge of both.

The two perspectives of parts and whole also indicate for Spinoza two complementary ways of talking about the universe. On the one hand, we speak about the universe as if it is something that's acted upon. For example, over the course of millions of years primates developed the ability to walk upright, use tools, and communicate using language. Here it sounds as if some outside force were manipulating the development of primates, resulting in the rise of modern humans. For Spinoza, speaking in this way would be speaking from the perspective of the parts. That is, speaking about the universe as if it were acted upon. Spinoza calls this perspective *natura naturata*, literally "natured nature." The great temptation, which Spinoza is wary of, is to ask, "If the universe is being acted upon, if nature is being natured, who's doing the acting, who's doing the naturing?" The traditional answer is, of course, God. But, God here is thought in the theistic sense of an entity that lies beyond the bounds of and limits the universe. As we've seen above, such a notion is incomprehensible to Spinoza. Either God must be thought of as identical to the universe, or God and the universe cannot interact with one another. Spinoza chooses pantheism over an infinitely distant and unthinkable God. This returns us to our original question though, "What's acting here?" The answer for Spinoza is simply the universe. Insofar as the universe acts it is considered *natura naturans*, or "naturing nature."

This seems to create more problems than it solves. Does this mean that the universe wills? Does the universe have its own designs and plans? If it does, how does this differ from theism, except in Spinoza's adamant contention that God and the universe are identical? It is not the case that for any effect we must think of the cause as originating in an agent separate from the effect. If I scratch an itch, then I (or at least part of me) is clearly acted upon. At the same time, however, I'm still the one doing the scratching. In this case, I don't assume that the itch or the scratching of it originate outside of me. I am both actor and acted upon. In the case of primate evolution above, it's easy to imagine the primates being acted upon over the course of millennia, but where's the acting? We wouldn't want to say that primates consciously brought about their own evolution. Rather, we say that evolution occurs through the processes of adaptation, mutation, and reproductive isolation that the primates are unaware of. Through these processes the flow of genetic material is governed, producing a variety of different types of primate and ultimately humans. The governing of genetic material through history, however, is not random but follows certain patterns, certain laws. It is through these laws that the universe acts on itself. Or, when we speak about nature acting, what we mean is that the universe is a lawful place, and that everything acts according to these laws. This is the way for Spinoza that nature natures.

What exactly are these laws by which the universe can be said to act? There are two basic kinds of laws for Spinoza, and these laws correspond to the attributes of substance. There are laws that govern the world insofar as it is perceived under the attribute of extension, that is, insofar as we take the universe to contain physical objects. These are the laws of physics. There are also laws that govern the world insofar as it is perceived under the attribute of thought, that is, insofar as we take the universe to contain mental objects. These are the laws of logic. (We'll explore this aspect in the next chapter.) For Spinoza both sets of laws have something essential in common. They are both kinds of causality, and causality is unthinkable without necessity. "From a given determinate cause the effect follows *necessarily*; and conversely, if there is no determinate cause, it is impossible for an effect to follow."[4] The laws of the universe, then, are the necessary connections of cause and effect that govern every relation in the universe, whether among the parts or between the parts and the whole.

For Spinoza, it is crucial that the connection between cause and effect be necessary. If it were possible that the exact same cause produce different effects, the universe would become incomprehensible. Nothing about it could be understood. If the ringing of a bell sometimes produced sound waves and sometimes did not, how would we ever come to terms with the nature of sound or human hearing? If dropping a pen sometimes resulted in the pen falling, but sometimes hovering or flying upward, would it make sense to talk about something like a law of gravity? In a situation where we cannot connect cause and effect with necessity, we cannot speak about laws at all. The same cause producing the same effect is the foundation of all scientific reasoning. All experimentation assumes the regularity of nature, that the same set of conditions will produce the same results every time. If an experiment is not repeatable the assumption is that there's an unaccounted for variable that is affecting the results. Or in Spinoza's terms, if the effect doesn't follow with necessity, it's because the cause has not been fully determined. Thus, for Spinoza every effect has a determinate cause such that the relation between cause and effect is one of necessity.

It is tempting to object at this point that Spinoza is working with an outmoded conception of causality, that advances in science such as quantum mechanics and chaos theory show that effects do not follow their causes with necessity. While it is certainly the case that notions of causality have undergone great changes, particularly in the latter half of the twentieth century, nevertheless, I think Spinoza's basic assumption still holds. Though we cannot predict with certainty both the speed and position of a subatomic particle, it does not follow from this that the speed and position of the particle are *uncaused*. The only thing that follows from this is that we don't know enough about subatomic particles to fully understand what they're capable of. Chaos theory also seems to introduce a disconnect between cause and effect such that they are no longer related necessarily. But, the claims of chaos theory (even the very name) are placeholders for our ignorance, rather than an indication that for very large systems effects do not necessarily follow their causes. If there really were chaos, then there could not be a theory of it, because theories depend on the necessary relation of cause and effect. It's perfectly plausible (even likely) that as finite entities there are things about the universe that we do not understand. It would be foolish in the highest degree, though, to suppose that something conclusive about the universe as a whole followed from our ignorance.

Spinoza's big picture seems to have taken us very far afield. Even if we agree with Spinoza that there can only be one substance, that attributes are ways of perceiving substance, and that modes are finite expressions of substance, this seems unrelated to the way I live my life. As we saw in the first chapter, though, the path of wisdom lies in understanding. The key to replacing passive affects with active ones lies in comprehending why something is the case. For Spinoza, the ultimate why is the big picture itself. All understanding flows from an understanding of the whole. But, as we saw, an understanding of the whole supposes that we see it as lawful. Without the necessary connection of cause and effect not only does any particular understanding become impossible, but it becomes impossible to see the big picture. Without lawful necessity one can see neither the forest nor the trees, so to speak. What remains to be seen, however, is how Spinoza's metaphysics (his big picture) affects his conception of the human mind. We saw above that thought is one of the attributes of substance and that thought works according to the laws of logic, but we did not flesh that out. In the next chapter we'll explore Spinoza's conception of mind. Once we have these pieces in place we'll be able to answer more fully how we overcome bondage and walk the path of wisdom.

NOTES

1. IA1.
2. ID4.
3. ID5.
4. IA3, emphasis added.

Chapter 5
What is mind? No matter.
What is matter? Never mind.

Before the Simpsons got their own show, they were a series of animated shorts on another show. In the very first appearance of the Simpsons, Homer is tucking Bart into bed and Bart asks, "Dad, what is the mind? Is it just a system of impulses or is it something tangible?" To which Homer replies, "Relax. What is mind? No matter. What is matter? Never mind." Unwittingly, as usual, Homer puts his finger on the exact problem that Spinoza is trying to solve in the second part of the *Ethics*. What is the mind, and what is its relation to matter? We already know that Spinoza finds Descartes' solution unworkable. There cannot be two substances, one that contains thoughts and one that contains extended things. This solution makes the nature of communication between mind and body incomprehensible. As we saw in the previous chapter, Spinoza solves the communication problem by arguing that both mind and matter belong to the same substance but are expressions of different attributes of this substance. Our task in this chapter will be to explore exactly how this works. In doing so we'll touch on issues in contemporary psychology as well as Spinoza's theory of knowledge, his epistemology. All of this, though, will be with a view to answering very practical questions about how one might walk the path of wisdom.

On the relation between mind and matter, it is not entirely clear that Spinoza has solved anything. Hasn't he simply redescribed the problem? What is the difference between having two substances and having two attributes of the same substance? Doesn't a fundamental duality remain? Aren't the attributes of thought and extension as radically separated as the substances thought and extension? Isn't some kind of mediation still required between mind and matter? Don't we still need the impossible object that is both mind and matter, something as absurd as Descartes' "animal spirits"? We can imagine Descartes smirking in the background saying, "See, I told you, it's not so easy." What Descartes has on his side are two overpowering intuitions that he lends further strength to. First, most people would take it as common sense that the mind is something radically different from the body. Descartes agrees and goes about giving philosophical support for this. The second, and even more obvious intuition, is that no matter how different mind and body are, they communicate. Demonstrating this is simplicity itself. I need only to think the (non-material) thought, "Lift your hand and scratch your head," which is then followed by the action of my (material) hand moving through (material) space and scratching my (material) head. Even the way we speak about these things lends support to Descartes' position. Notice when I describe my thought, it is in the first person, but when I describe my thought in relation to my body, my body is referred to in the second person, as if my thoughts were the real me and my body while part of me is separate from my mind. So, Descartes already has common sense on his side. The only thing he is missing is a mechanism that explains the way we already experience the world. Here Descartes fails, as his earliest critics point out, but the way we experience the world still seems to be in fundamental agreement with Descartes.

Spinoza is left in the awkward position of trying to account for our experience, but at the same time showing that the inference that Descartes draws from our experience is wrongheaded. His initial attempt does not seem promising, as it appears that Spinoza makes a distinction without a difference from two substances to two attributes. His difficulty is further exacerbated by the fact that for Spinoza attributes can no more interact with one another than can substances. For example, suppose I imagine some of the properties of a table, that it's brown and that its surface is about thirty inches off the ground. If I ask how these properties relate to one another, it seems the most I can say is they are both properties of the same table. Do the height and color interact with one another? Is one the cause of the other? Does the brownness cause the height or *vice versa*? The answer is emphatically, "No." The color and height of the table are unrelated causally. This is analogous to the relation between substance (table) and attributes (color and height) in Spinoza. The attributes of thought and extension belong to the same substance, but they cannot interact with one another.

Now Spinoza is in really big trouble. Not only is it not clear how he really differs from Descartes, but now he seems to be claiming that thoughts cannot affect bodies and bodies cannot affect thoughts. But, isn't it obviously the case that thoughts affect bodies? Right now as I write this, don't my thoughts have a causal relation to my fingers on the keyboard? Doesn't the clicking sound made by the keyboard cause the thought, "I hear the keyboard clicking"? The first thing we need to do to get Spinoza out of this mess is recall that attributes are not things; they are "ways of perceiving substance." So the issue here is not how do two unrelated *things* relate, but how do two ways of perceiving relate? Thus, the error of common sense is to suppose that mind and body are different *things*, and then ask about a mechanism for their causal relation. This is the clear difference between Spinoza and Descartes and the source of their different accounts of the mind.

The fact that attributes are not things but ways of perceiving substance leads us to the second way that Spinoza extricates himself from the difficulties imposed by our common sense and Descartes' argument. Different ways of perceiving do not require us to posit separate objects to be perceived. The same object can be perceived in multiple ways. Thus, for example, we talked about the differing perspectives that a physicist and a novelist might have on the world. There is no requirement that each must be talking about a different world. Or, we could imagine the way that a botanist and a poet might talk about the same rose. Both would have a different perspective on the same object. It wouldn't occur to us to wonder which perspective caused the other, or if one discourse might have an effect on the other. Rather, we would rightly suppose that these are two independent discourses about the same thing. In the same way, the attributes of thought and extension are two different ways of talking about the same substance. Furthermore, since every object is part of the same substance, every part of substance can also be perceived in these two different ways.

In order to illustrate Spinoza's position here, let's imagine that I'm walking around in flip-flops. As I walk into a room, I'm not watching where I'm going, and I accidentally catch my big toe underneath the half-opened door. This has the unfortunate consequence of bending my toenail back the wrong way and separating it slightly from the skin underneath. If Spinoza is right, I should be able to tell two stories about this event. One story would be purely material from the attribute of extension, and one story would be purely mental from the attribute of thought. While both stories need to be complete, neither story can intervene in the other. Thoughts and matter cannot be causally related to one another. The material story would go something like this: Two solid objects cannot occupy the same space at the same time. A collision between two solid objects results in the diminution of one or both. The diminution of a human toe causes the firing of nerve cells. The signal from these nerve cells travels up the leg to the spinal cord, where it causes C-fibers to fire in the brain. The firing of C-fibers sends signals back down the spinal column to the leg and foot, while adrenaline is released into the blood stream. Blood flow increases to the damaged area. At the same time my vocal chords let out an involuntary yelp in addition to a few choice words. Finally, this firing of C-fibers causes the grabbing of the foot and a careful observation of the damaged area. Notice first of all that the story of the event told here is completely physical, the interaction of a neuro-chemical system with a very hard object. Second, notice, in line with what we saw in the previous chapter, that all of the effects follow their causes with necessity. Damage to a human body does *necessarily* send nerve impulses to the brain, which causes C-fibers to fire. Now we can certainly imagine someone so stoically constituted that suddenly losing a toenail does not result in yelping or swearing, but the only change we would make to the physical story is that C-fibers firing are not a sufficient cause for such behavior.

We normally do not speak about C-fibers firing. We speak about pain. In fact, and this is where the confusion arises, we speak about the mental state pain as the cause of physical effects, such as yelping or hopping up and down. For Spinoza this is to confuse two orders of discourse, and it is precisely this confusion of ways of perceiving that lead to Descartes' error and requires us to account for the relation of two things that are unrelated. For Spinoza we do justice to the mental way of perceiving things by not confusing it with the material way of perceiving things. So, in the case of stubbing my toe, thinking this event under the attribute of thought would go like this: The idea of stubbing my toe is followed by the idea of pain, which is followed by hatred of the door and anger at my stupidity. These ideas are all followed by the ideas of hopping up and down and swearing loudly. The idea of pain also causes me to think about sitting down in order to get an idea of how damaged my foot is. Perceived in this way, stubbing my toe is understood purely as a concatenation of ideas. One idea leads to another idea. Ideas never cause anything physical. The causality of ideas is only related to other ideas, and for Spinoza the causal relation among ideas is just as necessary as the causal relation among physical objects. Someone no doubt might object that none of these ideas would have arisen if you hadn't stubbed your toe, so the physical is clearly having an effect on the mental. This is where Descartes' position is so insidious. The objection begs the question. It assumes that the mental and physical are two different *things* and therefore assumes that a causal relation is possible between them. Spinoza's position avoids this difficulty by arguing that there are not two things at stake here but two ways of describing the same thing, and that different ways of describing manifestly do not relate to one another causally. Thus, stubbing my toe does not cause the idea of pain. Stubbing my toe causes C-fibers to fire. At the same time, an idea of stubbing my toe is followed necessarily by an idea of pain. But, C-fibers firing and the idea of pain are not two separate things, so one doesn't cause the other. Rather, C-fibers firing and the idea of pain are the same thing talked about in two different ways, like the botanist and the poet talking about the same rose.

Spinoza, thus, completely dissolves the issue of how mind and body relate. The problem arises only when we assume that mind and body are separate things. If, in contrast to this, we suppose that humans are complex individuals that relate to the world in complex ways, and that one may account for these relations in two irreducible ways, then we get a new perspective on humanity in general. There is no longer a need to privilege the mind over the body, as has been the tendency for the greater part of Western thought, nor is it even possible. Mind and body are simply different stories we tell about the same object.

While I have been at pains to distinguish thought and extension as ways of perceiving that do not relate to one another causally, there is an important way that thought and extension are alike. Spinoza writes that the "order and connection of ideas is the same as the order and connection of things."[1] Although it may look as though Spinoza is abandoning his rigorous distinction between mind and matter here, a closer look reveals that he is not. His claim is not that ideas and things are identical or interact in any way but that their order of connection is the same. This, of course, raises the question, what does Spinoza mean by "order of connection"? If ideas and things are separate, how can they have something that's the same, even an order of connection? Spinoza has two things in mind here. First, since ideas and things are two ways of talking about the same thing, the order of events remains unchanged. Thus, in the order of connection among things, the firing of C-fibers comes after damage to the toe. In the same way that in the order of connection among ideas, the idea of pain follows the idea of stubbing one's toe. The two stories are parallel to one another, precisely because they're stories about a single event.

The second thing that Spinoza has in mind by sameness of order of connection is necessity. The necessity of physical connections is easy for us to conceive. We are used to thinking chemical reactions as being necessary. Given the right set of chemical precursors, the same result always follows. We are less used to thinking about thoughts in terms of necessary causality, though. Isn't it obvious that we flit from thought to thought, that thoughts continually come to us unbidden without precursor? Aren't we surprised by our fantasies and dreams? For Spinoza this is another case of confusing ignorance with randomness. Just because we don't know why a particular thought enters our mind, doesn't mean it's uncaused. I often have the experience of being in a long conversation, and though the conversation usually starts out on some heady topic of philosophy, I find myself talking about something ridiculous by comparison, say the relative merits of one kind of deodorant over another. Often in these conversations, both my conversation partner and I will stop and look at each other and say, "Why are we talking about this?" When this question arises, it has never been the case that we say, "Oh, it's just random." No, we begin thinking about the development of the conversation and usually we're able to come up with the crucial turning points in the conversation. Philosophy led to Nietzsche, which led to Nietzsche's concern about smell, this caused one of us to mention being stuck in a tight space with someone who smelled, which led to a discussion of deodorants. Thoughts aren't any more random than the relation of physical objects, though they often seem more random because we don't always take the time to retrace the steps of our thoughts. Or, sometimes the causes of our thoughts remain unconscious to us, and this is the insight that animates psychoanalysis. We might be subtly shaped by childhood events that we have forgotten and so the thoughts generated by these causes cannot be so easily traced. For Spinoza, no matter how convoluted our thoughts seem, there is always an underlying logic.

The fact that the order of the connection of our thoughts is necessary brings us to Spinoza's theory of knowledge. The first type of knowledge for Spinoza is knowledge that is dependent on images. By this he means both information gleaned from our senses and information gleaned from others through hearing, reading, or memory. While most people would call this "knowledge" and Spinoza follows suit, he does not think that it's real knowledge, and thus calls it "opinion." The reason that it's not real knowledge is because it uses images to compensate for the limitations of our imagination. If I see a particular dog, its uniqueness stands out. After seeing five dogs, the uniqueness of each begins to fade. At a hundred dogs, it becomes exceedingly difficult to talk about individual dogs. In order to compensate for my limits here I invent the universal "dog," which refers to all dogs indeterminately. There are two problems with this. First, the universal lies. It cannot capture the uniqueness of individual dogs, and the fact of the matter is we do not imagine a universal dog; we only have images of particular dogs. Second, our universals are dependent on our bodily disposition. If I am inclined to like bigger dogs with short but not curly hair, my universal will reflect that. If another person is inclined to fear dogs and think them vicious and dirty, his universal will reflect that. The fact that universals obscure what they claim to explain and that different people produce different universals is the reason why so much controversy exists. We argue by defending our universal against others. But, even if we win the argument, we've gained nothing. We've only proved that one figment of the imagination is superior to another figment of the imagination.

The second kind of knowledge concerns "common notions and adequate ideas of the properties of things."[2] At the outset "common notion" seems uncomfortably close to "universal," which Spinoza was so critical of above. However, Spinoza does recognize that, while there is no universal dog, it is still the case that since everything is part of the same universe, these parts will necessarily share some properties. The kinds of properties that Spinoza has in mind here are things like objects, though under the attribute of extension, all take up space. Furthermore, all spatial objects will share additional properties that are codified in geometry. Notice that these common notions do not depend on a universal like dog, but look at the properties of individual things and ask if other individual things have the same property. Common notions are thus transversal; that is, they cut across the strict boundaries that we draw with our universals and ask what unique individuals have in common. Furthermore, since these common notions concern the actual properties of actual objects, we move from inadequate ideas about things to adequate ideas about things. In the case of universals created by my imagination, the universal intervenes between me and the individual. As a result, I can easily make a false conclusion. Thus, if my universal dog includes the bromide "man's (yet another universal) best friend (also a universal)" I will not understand why I'm bitten by this particular dog. If, on the other hand, I think about this particular dog in terms of a several sets of properties that intersect at the nexus of dog, environment, and me, some of which I have common notions, a true conclusion is much more likely. Even if I misapprehend the situation, though, it will not be because I have an inaccurate universal. It will be because I do not have an adequate idea of some of the properties at play here.

Spinoza calls this type of knowledge "reason." He calls it "reason" because it deals in adequate ideas. As we saw above, an adequate idea is one in which everything that it entails is clear. For example, an adequate idea of a triangle entails that its interior angles are equal to two right angles. If my idea of triangle does not include this, then I am bound to make false conclusions about triangles. However, to the degree that my idea does include a true claim, any additional claims that follow from this are also true. Adequate ideas are true and connected to one another with necessity. Reason thus sees the necessary connection among individual things. In contrast to this, ideas based on universals, or the imagination, are necessarily inadequate. They are inadequate because through them we are unable to comprehend what follows with necessity. So, for example, though my universal dog is a large, short-haired dog with four legs, it does not follow that all actual dogs have four legs. Nor does it follow that all dogs are large or have short hair. Precisely because these universals are inadequate, precisely because we cannot get necessity out of them, they only appear to be knowledge and are not actual knowledge. Since reason deals in necessity, it is true knowledge.

The third kind of knowledge also deals in necessity, so it is a true kind of knowledge. But, there is also a crucial difference. Spinoza calls it "intuitive knowledge" and says that, "this kind of knowing proceeds from an adequate idea of the formal essence of certain attributes of [the universe] to the adequate knowledge of the essence of things."[3] The easiest way to talk about the difference between reason and intuitive knowledge is to return to the parts and whole or the trees and forest language of the previous chapter. In these terms we could say that reason had an adequate idea of the parts and thus sees the necessary connection among the parts. Reason moves from tree to tree, so to speak. In contrast to this, intuitive knowledge proceeds from an adequate idea of the whole (from one of the attributes of substance) to an adequate idea of the parts. Intuitive knowledge moves from the forest to the trees, as it were. What we gain in intuitive knowledge is a grasp of the big picture as the necessary connection of all the parts to the whole. We see that everything that is follows from the nature of the universe. For any particular thing to be different than it is now would require that the universe as a whole were different and operated according to different laws. Intuitive knowledge sees things from the perspective of *natura naturans* (naturing nature, the whole), while reason sees things from the perspective of *natura naturata* (natured nature, the parts).

This view of the universe insofar as it is an active whole bringing about the changes in its parts according to necessary laws Spinoza calls "*sub specie aeternitatis*" or under the aspect of eternity. The temptation here is to turn this into a theistic "God's eye view," but the only thing Spinoza has in mind here is that it is possible to view the world in its constant changes from the perspective of that which does not change. The unchanging here does not refer to a transcendent God over and above creation, but to that which makes the change possible, namely the laws that govern the universe. Take triangles, for example. While we can imagine a nearly infinite number of triangles and could produce many of them over a given period of time, their production is governed by a set of laws about the enclosure of space in simple plane objects. These laws, which follow necessarily from the universe thought under that attribute of extension, are eternal. They remain unchanged by the production of triangles in history.

Spinoza's theory of knowledge returns us to the practical problem of understanding. If being myself depends on my understanding of why something happened to me, then it is clear in the first instance that this understanding cannot involve the first kind of knowledge. Insofar as my thoughts are dominated by images, universals, I fail to grasp things adequately. "Knowledge of the first kind is the only cause of falsity."[4] Every misconception that I have is the result of using universals in place of "adequate ideas of the properties of things." The result of thinking in universals is that I fail to understand myself and the world, insofar as I do not understand I am in bondage. In contrast to this, Spinoza holds up the second and third kinds of knowledge as "necessarily true." Whatever Spinoza means by understanding, then, must be related to these types of true knowledge. The replacement of passive affects with active ones must be the result of thinking in terms of reason and intuitive knowledge. As we saw, what these two kinds of knowledge have in common is seeing the necessary connection, either among the parts or between the whole and the parts. In the next chapter, we'll explore the difficult relation between this necessity and true freedom.

NOTES

1. IIP7.
2. IIP40S2.
3. IIP40S2.
4. IIP41.

Chapter 6
True Freedom

Spinoza's insistence that the type of understanding needed to free oneself from bondage is intimately related to necessity is initially unproblematic. Surely, we expect physicists, mathematicians, and biologists to pursue the necessary connection of events, even if their knowledge is not always sufficient to realize it. Furthermore, we tacitly depend on precisely this necessity in our everyday lives. We do not walk off very tall buildings in the hope that gravity may not apply. We expect gravity to apply every time without exception, necessarily. Our activities are organized around this expectation, this necessity. While we happily rely on necessity for our basic movements, and happily accept scientific explanations of the universe and everything in it in terms of necessity, there is one crucial realm that we reserve as immune from necessity: the human will. We are more adamant that the human will is free than we are that the rest of the universe follows from necessity. This is where Spinoza's position becomes problematic to most people. He argues that free will is illusory, and that escape from bondage, true freedom, depends on ridding oneself of this illusion.

If free will is an illusion, how did it become so widespread? For Spinoza, an unshakeable belief in free will has several sources. The first of these sources is the conception of humans as a "kingdom within a kingdom." We analyzed this briefly in the second chapter. Humans believe that they operate under different rules from the rest of the universe. Chief among these different rules is a free will. Thus, while we can maintain that everything else in the universe follows necessarily, human will does not. In maintaining free will we usually do not reflect on the radicalism of the claim. What exactly does it mean for the will to be free? It would mean that the will is not subject to the same laws of causality as the rest of the universe. Everything else in the universe follows its cause with necessity, but this would not be so with the will. We must suppose that the effects of the will are inadequately caused. For Spinoza, this is tantamount to imagining an effect without a cause sufficient to determine it. Is it really plausible to think about effects without causes? We wouldn't allow it in any other domain, and Spinoza does not see why we should allow it in the case of the human will. At the very least, the burden of proof is on those who would argue that the will is free, despite thinking that nothing else in the universe is.

The second source of belief in free will is a dualism of mind and body. If one could demonstrate that the mind is separate from the physical universe, then it need not be subject to the same laws as the physical universe. Will as a component of mind could thus be free in such a system. As we saw in the previous chapter, though, a dualism of this type is untenable. A mind so separated from the body that it shares nothing in common with it, though conceivably operating according to different laws, cannot plausibly communicate with the body, because there would be no common medium through which each could communicate with the other. To solve this problem Spinoza proposes a monism in which mind and body are two different ways of talking about the same object. This solves the problem of communication by eliminating the positing of separate things that must communicate. However, what follows from this is the affirmation of the human mind within the universe and thus subject to the laws of the universe. As Spinoza claims, "the order and connection of ideas is the same as the order and connection of things."[1] What follows from this is the absolute determination of the will. Willing for Spinoza would simply be another thought necessarily caused by a long chain of thoughts. "The will cannot be called a free cause, but only a necessary one."[2] Everything in Spinoza's universe follows with necessity even human willing.

The third source of belief in free will, and the source that makes such a belief so intractable, is ignorance. The ignorance here is not simply ignorance about the nature of the will, but ignorance about one's own thought processes that foster the illusion of free will. "So experience itself, no less clearly than reason, teaches that men believe themselves free because they are conscious of their own actions, and ignorant of the causes by which they are determined."[3] Spinoza has no problem admitting that we often do not know why we do what we do. It does not therefore follow, though, that not knowing why something is done makes it random, free, or undetermined. As we've seen time and time again no conclusions can follow from ignorance. We would not want to base something seemingly so crucial to humanity as free will on something so flimsy as ignorance.

Some will argue that Spinoza has misunderstood free will. It must mean something other than he has in mind. He has erected a straw man here. Others will argue that even if we cannot defend it against Spinoza's attacks, it's too important to give up. Without free will, responsibility becomes meaningless. Without responsibility there can be no morality and no justice. If every action is determined, how can we hold anyone accountable for anything morally or legally? Given these concerns let's try to formulate a conception of will that avoids Spinoza's conclusions and at the same time avoids the pitfalls that brought on Spinoza's criticisms in the first place. Most would argue that freedom of the will lies in making the choices that give our life direction. Thus, we imagine life as a series of choices among possibilities that are completely undetermined. A senior in high school applies to a dozen universities and is accepted to four. Surely, she is free in her choice. Of course, she must take responsibility for her choice, but the choice is hers to make. Or, what about something more mundane? There are numerous ways I can return home from my office. There's a northern route, a southern route, and a middle route. Isn't it my free will that chooses one of these routes over another? Or, what about the case of road rage from chapter 1? Wasn't it my free choice to become angry? Couldn't I have just as easily thought about puppies or candy? Couldn't I have turned down a different street so as not to exacerbate my anger? As we examine these situations, our notion of what a free will is becomes clearer. By saying we freely choose among several possible options, the presupposition that underlies this is that given the same set of circumstances and the same choices, we could freely choose otherwise. This presupposition manifests itself in numerous ways, sometimes as pride in the case where a gamble pays off. "I could've played it safe, but I didn't. I took a risk and it paid off handsomely." Most of the time, though, this presupposition manifests itself as regret, because we don't spend as much time analyzing decisions that go well. "I wish I had gone to a different college, instead of the one I chose." In either case the assumption is if one could do things all over again one *could* do them differently. This seems to be at the heart of free will. It's here that both moral and legal responsibility lie. We are held responsible precisely because we could have acted otherwise.

Let's examine this presupposition using the movie *Groundhog Day*. The movie turns on the premise of one man, played by Bill Murray, living the same day over and over again. While the calendar doesn't progress, Bill Murray's character certainly does—from incomprehension to indifference to depression to acceptance. Many would argue that the development of his character proves that he is free. He is faced with the same set of circumstances over and over again and continually chooses otherwise, until he finally wakes up on February third. Closer inspection reveals, however, that this is not the only explanation for what's going on here. It appears that Bill Murray is choosing freely because in the face of the same circumstances he chooses differently. There is a crucial difference, though, in each of his Groundhog Days. Bill Murray *remembers* that this is the same day each time, and he *remembers* how many times he's already gone through this. This difference is sufficient to change the conditions under which Bill Murray chooses. As a point of comparison, note the way the other people in the movie act who do not remember that it is the same day over and over again. They act exactly the same every time, until Bill Murray interacts with them differently. This new interaction results in a different set of choices. The question that still remains, however, is whether or not the choice is free. Spinoza is adamant that this is not the case. In the case of the other characters in the movie, their choices are not free because in each case they could not have acted otherwise. When they had the same set of causes leading to a series of choices, their choice remains the same every time. When Bill Murray introduced a new cause, it's true they did make a different choice, but the reason for this new choice is very clear. They chose differently because of the new cause introduced by Murray. By the same token, while Bill Murray's character clearly undergoes a radical transformation in the movie, this transformation is precisely the *result* of his memory. If the movie had not introduced the conceit that all of this happens on the same day repeated *ad nauseum*, we would simply say that Bill Murray learned from his experience. That is, even though it appears that he is facing the same situation over and over again, he is crucially different. He remembers what happened the last time he was faced with the situation, and that knowledge causes him to act differently. His will is not free here but determined by what has happened in the past.

For example, when I turn the stove on and see the flash of the burner followed by the steady blue flame, I never stick my hand in the fire. Why? Because I freely choose not to? Or, because I have been told since a very young age that fire burns and beyond that I have actually been burned and have no desire to repeat the experience? This first explanation seems like a willful ignorance of who I am, what I know, and the habits that I've formed. Spinoza sees clearly that there is always a reason for what we do, even if we are not always conscious of that reason. It's these reasons that determine our will. The idea of fire is followed by the idea of being careful not to burn oneself. The connection between these two ideas has been forged over a lifetime of learning and experience, and they follow one another with the same necessity as the idea of dropping a pen from a height is followed by the idea of it falling. The order and connection of ideas is necessary and our will is not free from this necessity but a part of it. In contrast to the necessity that Spinoza argues for, the defenders of free will would have to claim that when faced with an open flame we sovereignly declare, "Even though in the same situation I *could* choose differently, today I choose not to be burned."

Spinoza's point is this: there are choices. We can see them arrayed before us. When we're suspended in this moment prior to the choice it seems as if they are all equally possible. This thus gives rise to the feeling that if faced with the same situation we could choose differently. The fact, though, that all of the choices seem equally possible arises from ignorance. My decision will ultimately be based on some reason, some necessary connection of ideas that will completely determine my will. If I do not understand the reason why I make one choice over another, my choice will appear random, and I could easily imagine making a different choice. Someone reading this book right now might be thinking, "I can either keep on reading, or I can stop. The choice is mine and there's nothing anyone can do about it." So far Spinoza would agree with this reasoning. His only point is that whether the reader stops or continues there will be a reason (not necessarily a good reason, but a reason nonetheless) that determines the will. Perhaps the reader planned to finish this chapter before doing something else. Perhaps the reader will throw down the book in disgust to prove a point. Spinoza will calmly point out that in both cases the will is determined either by the previous plan or the desire to prove a point. "Aha!" some will shout. Where did the plan to finish the chapter come from? Wasn't that the reader's free choice? It's true that the reader made a plan, but why did she make such a plan? Is she the type of person that makes plans? How did she get that way? Were her parents also planners? Did she learn an important lesson at some point when she failed to make plans? Spinoza wouldn't see any free will here, only the necessary connection of ideas necessarily determining the will. People don't *just* become planners or non-planners. They become such through a long chain of previous causes in which the effects follow with necessity. There is no randomness in Spinoza's universe, and the human will is not an exception to this. When we make a claim about randomness, we are actually making a claim about our ignorance.

Thus, on the one hand, Spinoza is adamant that the will is not free but determined necessarily by the thoughts that precede it. On the other hand, Spinoza does think that human freedom is possible. We are so accustomed to thinking that freedom belongs to the will that it is difficult to think of it in any other way. John Locke, a British philosopher and one generally opposed to Spinoza's way of doing philosophy provides some unexpected help in this regard. In his *Essay Concerning Human Understanding* (1690), which appears a dozen or so years after Spinoza's death, Locke deftly illustrates Spinoza's point. He asks us to imagine that during the night someone spirits us away, bed and all, to a locked room. In that locked room waits someone we would very much like to talk to, so that when we awaken we can spend our time in pleasant conversation. At this point, Locke asks two probing questions that get to the heart of the matter: 1) Would we will to be there talking to someone we would like to talk to? 2) In such a situation are we free? The answer to the first question is yes; we would choose to be in that room talking to the desired person. But, the answer to the second question is no; we are not free, because we cannot leave. Locke wonders how it is possible that we could be doing exactly what we want but be unfree. Isn't doing what one wants the definition of "freedom"? Locke's position is that if freedom and will can be clearly separated like this, they must not be related in the way that we think. His claim is that "freedom" does not properly modify "the will." To say "free will" is a categorical mistake. Rather, "freedom" is a claim about power. We would all agree that we are unfree in a locked room, because we do not have the *power* to leave.[4]

On this point, at least, Locke and Spinoza are in fundamental agreement. For Spinoza true freedom has to do with one's power rather than one's will. If we return to Spinoza's concluding remarks from the *Ethics* this becomes clear.

> With this I have finished all the things I wished to show concerning the mind's *power* over the affects and its freedom. From what has been shown, it is clear how much the wise man is capable of, and how much more *powerful* he is than one who is ignorant and is driven only by lust.[5]

Here we can see the clear connection between power and freedom and also where Spinoza would differ from Locke. For Locke freedom is simply the absence of physical constraint, but for Spinoza freedom involves the mind exerting power over its affects. The ability to exert power over one's affects is precisely what distinguishes the wise from the foolish.

At this point, no doubt, objections come pouring in. How can we have power over our affects if everything is determined? Don't we need free will to *choose* to exert power over our affects? Or, if our choices are completely determined by the thoughts that preceded those choices, where does the power lie? Doesn't Spinoza just turn us into pawns at the mercy of our past and the world? The objections posed here certainly see the radicalism of Spinoza's ethical project. They rightly see that all of the notions on which we believe morality depends—such as free will, guilt, and responsibility—are eviscerated by Spinoza. At the same time, however, these questions also presuppose that free will, guilt, and responsibility must still be operative in Spinoza's system. It is profoundly difficult to give up one's belief in free will. This belief, however, is precisely what prevents one from having power over one's affects.

Let's examine how belief in free will actually gives one less power over one's affects rather than more. In the case of road rage from the first chapter, what is animating my anger? On the surface, my anger is animated by the fact that I've been cut off. It can't merely be the fact that I've been cut off, though. Being cut off in itself doesn't necessarily give rise to anger. If I'm cut off by a fire engine with its lights on, I don't get angry. Also, when I discover that the SUV driver is taking a pregnant passenger to the hospital, I'm no longer angry. So, if it's not being cut off in itself that stirs my wrath, what is it? Our initial temptation is to say that sometimes it's justifiable to cut people off, say, in cases of emergency. This seems unhelpful, though; we rarely know why people cut us off. In those cases we're left wondering if this case is justified and usually concluding that it is not, thus leading to anger. But, anger is one of those instances where our affects have power over us. We are foolish when we are angry, not wise. Furthermore, we don't get to the real source of the anger. I was angry at the SUV driver, because I believed he freely chose to cut me off. Or, he didn't have to cut me off. He could've acted otherwise. It's thus my assumption that in that situation the SUV driver could have acted otherwise, could have seen the possibilities laid out before him and freely chosen the one that didn't inconvenience me. When I see the driver pull into the hospital, though, certainly I understand why I was cut off, but what exactly do I understand at that moment? I understand that, though, hypothetically the SUV driver had multiple choices, he had reasons that completely determined him to drive as he did. Thus, I can only be angry at the SUV driver to the extent that I believe he has free will and has freely chosen to cut me off. The second I understand that his choice was not free but determined by previous choices, habits, and knowledge, I am no longer angry.

At this point, we come to the limits of the road rage example. The obvious objection here is that I've stacked the deck. The illustration only works because I know why the guy cut me off, and it seems to be a legitimate reason. So, let's modify the example. Let's say that I don't know why the guy is cutting me off. Let's also say that I've come across the same SUV on multiple occasions around town, and he cuts me off every time. Furthermore, let's say that it appears that the SUV driver appears to take a perverse glee in cutting me off. It's as if he sees me coming, smiles, and then cuts me off. In short, this guy is a jerk. Shouldn't I do something about this? Isn't it right to get angry here? Why should I be a doormat for this guy? How can I have power if I let him walk all over me like that? Spinoza is clear that anytime some external cause is the source of our thoughts we are in bondage and not free. To the degree that I'm angry at this guy, he colonizes my thoughts. My thoughts are no longer my own, but can only be explained through my interactions with this guy. If someone else is the cause of my thoughts, if my thoughts are not my own, I cannot be free; I cannot be wise.

Instead of cooking up another delicious revenge fantasy, let's step back from this situation and think about it. The first question that comes to mind is, why is this guy being a jerk? Did I do something? Where does this animosity come from? Ultimately, these are dead-end questions. I'll probably never know why this guy is a jerk, or where the seeming animosity comes from. But, if I alter the question slightly to, could this guy be anything other than a jerk? Or, should I assume that he freely chose to be a jerk? This sends my inquiry into a completely different direction. This guy is a jerk right now because he is determined to be so by previous choices, habits, and knowledge, which were themselves determined by even more remote causes all the way back to the beginning of the universe. He is currently the way he is because he cannot be otherwise, or to imagine a universe in which this guy is not a jerk is to imagine a different universe with different laws. Furthermore, if I think about why I keep running into this guy all over town, the results are very similar. The reason I live in this town, drive on these roads, drive the way that I do is the result of an infinite chain of antecedent causes that could not be otherwise. Thus, my interaction with this jerk is not mere happenstance that goes badly when one of the actors freely chooses to act in an untoward manner. No, our interaction is the necessary result of causes that stretch back to the beginning of time. Our being there at that time, his being a jerk are no less necessary than the sum of a triangle's interior angles being equal to two right angles. When seen in this light, what exactly is there to be angry about? Everything is following the laws of nature with necessity. I should no more get angry about this than I would get about water getting me wet. I never reproach the water for getting me wet. I never imagine that the water could do anything other than get me wet. That's its nature.

Spinoza's claim at this point, though, is not that we become doormats and let everyone walk all over us, because that's their nature. His claim is that nothing productive will arise from anger. Insofar as I am angry I will not act in a way that benefits me or others. Spinoza is not arguing for pacifism here, but understanding. His claim is we can only truly act to the degree that we are ourselves, but we cannot act when overwhelmed by emotions contrary to our nature.

Spinoza thus leaves us with the paradoxical claim that my freedom lies in understanding the necessity of things. How precisely does this work? Notice in the example above, it was only to the degree that I assumed the SUV driver could have acted otherwise that my anger was roused. But, insofar as my anger is roused, I am not myself. At that point I've just entered into a combination with an external object that weakens me, that is toxic to me. It is toxic precisely because my thoughts are no longer my own. They are sidetracked by this unhealthy intrusion. The power of my mind is obviously greater when it is not distracted. I find it very difficult to write when I am upset by something. What I'm upset about keeps redirecting my thoughts, taking them down dark paths. Supposing that we grant Spinoza's claim, what is the antidote to this toxicity? It cannot be that by force of will I freely choose to think otherwise. What then? I neutralize the effects of combining with something opposed to my nature by recognizing that its opposition to my nature is just as necessary as my interacting with it at this point. It is the very recognition of the necessity of all things that neutralizes an opposing cause's toxicity. When I recognize that neither I nor the jerk could have acted otherwise, and that our meeting is the result of the same necessity, my initial anger is transformed. I replace the passive affects predicated on an external cause and replace them with the active affects of my own striving. A cause for anger now becomes a cause for understanding the nature of the universe. This is what Spinoza calls "intuitive knowledge" or "the third kind of knowledge." It is the key to the path of wisdom.

> He who rightly knows that all things follow from the necessity of [the universe], and happen according to the eternal laws and rules of nature, will surely find nothing worthy of hate, mockery or disdain, nor anyone whom he will pity. Instead he will strive, as far as human virtue allows, to act well, as they say, and rejoice.[6]

I can only be myself when I am free. I can only be free when I understand that things could not be otherwise. The minute I begin thinking that things could be otherwise, I find myself combined with external causes in the most damaging ways. I begin to hate, mock, and pity. When I understand the necessity of all things, my thoughts and actions are my own. I combine with things that agree with rather than oppose my nature. This is blessedness (*beatitudo*); this is true freedom.

NOTES

1. IIP7.
2. IP32.

3. IIIP2S.

4. John Locke, *Essay Concerning Human Understanding* in *The Empiricists* (New York: Doubleday, 1961), 44.

5. VP42S, emphasis added.

6. IVP50S.

Chapter 7
Bodies in Motion

Now that we have seen what freedom means for Spinoza, we can use this as a base to pursue additional practical matters. Before we pursue these issues in any depth, though, we need to look more closely at Spinoza's conception of a body so that we can think more clearly about the ways bodies interact. Spinoza's discussion of bodies is found in part II of the *Ethics*. As we saw above, body and mind are not opposed to one another but two ways of talking about a single individual. Thus, talking about the relation of an individual's thoughts to one another is perceiving the individual under the attribute of thought. And, talking about the ways in which an individual physically interacts with herself and her environment is perceiving the individual under the attribute of extension. It is in this context that a discussion of bodies arises. Given that we are part of a greater whole, how can we understand our place in the universe in purely physical terms? How can we think ourselves as bodies in space? This, of course, does not deny that we can also be thought as a necessary concatenation of thoughts, but both ways of understanding must be fully explicated.

The discussion of bodies in part II of the *Ethics* represents a departure of form for Spinoza. Though, he remains with Euclid's terminology for demonstration, here he introduces an apparatus of new axioms, "lemmas," and "postulates" that is not repeated elsewhere in the book. Having demonstrated that an individual's thoughts necessarily begin with his body in the propositions leading up to this point, Spinoza turns to the body itself in a series of postulates that are set apart from (though not unrelated to) what preceded it. It is difficult to overestimate how prescient Spinoza is in this section. Far from marking him as a relic of a bygone era, many of these claims are in line with our most recent advances in neuroscience.[1]

We learn several important things about bodies from Spinoza's account. In the first set of axioms we see that bodies are always at motion or at rest, and that those in motion move at different speeds. From this follows the first claim about distinguishing one body from another. "Bodies are distinguished from one another by reason of motion and rest, speed and slowness, and not by reason of substance."[2] While the claim here seems innocent enough, it is actually a devastating challenge to most traditional theories of knowledge. The theories of knowledge that Spinoza would have been familiar with usually distinguished objects in terms of separate substances. In these terms, the phone is not a plant because each has different properties that inhere in different substances. Of course, for Spinoza there is only one substance, so objects can't be distinguished in this way. Rather, Spinoza distinguishes bodies in terms of their speed and whether they're at motion or rest. Once we learn more about bodies, we'll illustrate this further, but for now suffice it to say that what Spinoza is proposing is a relational model of knowledge whereby everything is defined by its relation to the objects around it, and that this definition does not depend on individual substances but motion and speed.

The next important thing we learn about bodies is that a body is more or less complex depending on the number of parts that it has. Thus, single-celled organisms are very simple bodies, because they have very few parts. Jellyfish are more complex, because they have more parts. One could even say that insofar as a jellyfish is organized into differing parts—locomotion, predation, digestion—it is composed of a number of different individuals that are related as a whole. In this respect a "human body is composed of a great many individuals of different natures, each of which is highly composite."[3] Thus, Spinoza sees the universe as composed of parts that organize themselves into individuals, which then organize themselves into even more complex individuals, all according to the laws of the universe. These individuals are not themselves distinct substances, which would by definition prevent their interactions with other individuals. These individuals are rather temporary coagulations of diverse parts that compose themselves for a time and then ultimately decompose to form new combinations. This is the nature of the universe. This is life and death, and Spinoza explains it without resorting to the problematic idea of individual substances.

The third thing we learn about bodies is that complex bodies, a human body for example, are a "ratio of motion and rest" among their parts. Thus, while Spinoza's previous point accounts for change, this point accounts for stability. The parts that compose a body can only form a body to the degree that they agree in some respect. This agreement takes the form of a ratio. My arm, for example, is joined to my torso at my shoulder. This joining makes certain motions possible, but others impossible—impossible in the sense that if I exceed that range of motion my shoulder will become dislocated, disturbing the ratio of motion and rest between arm and torso. The ratio of motion and rest among the parts of my body determine the ways I can affect and be affected, and which other bodies disturb or preserve my ratio of motion and rest. Thus, while salt is deadly if it touches a slug, it has no effect on me. By the same token, a flu virus that radically diminishes my capacities would have no effect on the slug.

Notice here how Spinoza's understanding of the body quickly returns us to a discussion of affects. For Spinoza what determines the ways that a body affects and is affected is the ratio of motion and rest among its parts. In some cases we call these affects emotions, but as we've seen all along the affects are much broader than this. Stubbing my toe is also a way of being affected and this is made possible by the particular way that my body is put together.

In order to tie together these disparate aspects of a body, let's borrow an example from another commentator.[4] Since human bodies are very complex, let's use something a little simpler, a tick. Ticks have eight legs and feed by sucking the blood from warm-blooded creatures. What makes a tick what it is? The traditional answer would be to locate the tick in a larger taxonomy. So, ticks are a kind of arachnid, the group that also contains scorpions and spiders. The reason that ticks are grouped here is that all the members of the group (usually) have eight legs and subsist on a liquid diet. Of course, the nature of this liquid diet and the way it is acquired is radically different in each case. Spiders and scorpions (usually) inject a toxin that dissolves the inside of their prey into a liquid they then drink. Ticks, in contrast, drink blood directly from the host and do not inject any venom. Furthermore, ticks have a parasitical relation to their sustenance, not a predatory one.

A taxonomy of this type simply repeats the kind of substance metaphysics that Spinoza was arguing against. It assumes that there is some substance "arachnidness" that each of these creatures exemplifies and on which the stability of the species depends. Spinoza would argue that the way one could more helpfully understand the tick is in terms of the particular way its parts are joined together in a particular individual (i.e., its ratio of motion and rest) and the affects that this makes possible. A tick has a torso with a hard shell, a small head, and relatively long legs in relation to its body. It is sensitive to light, and its body can expand as it ingests blood. These parts stand in a certain relation to one another, and thus make some affects possible while precluding others. The tick, for example, is not so composed that it can fly. But, it is composed so that it can climb toward the light, fall on warm-blooded creatures, burrow through fur, and suck blood. If it had different parts, or a different ratio among parts, these affects would not be possible. Longer legs might make climbing easier but might prevent burrowing through fur undetected. A larger body might hold more blood but might make falling on a host problematic. So, not only do the ratio of motion and rest among the parts of the tick make certain affects possible, but these affects will be exercised to a certain degree of intensity. A tick unable to exercise any of its affects will enter a period of hibernation in order to preserve as long as possible its ratio of motion and rest. At the other end of the spectrum, a tick fully gorged on the blood of its host has exercised all of its affects to the maximal degree, at which point it disengages from the host to start the process all over. These two aspects, the affects made possible by the ratio of motion and rest among the parts and the degree to which these affects are exercised, form a coordinate system on which we might define a tick. The affects give a latitudinal coordinate and their degree of engagement gives a longitudinal coordinate. We'll return to this idea again in the chapter on the environment, but for now we can say that Spinoza gives us a way of understanding a body that is not dependent on what he calls "universals" or the first kind of knowledge, but arise directly out of the thing itself.

We can thus imagine Spinoza's universe as an enormous billiard table on which the motion of one ball is transferred to another ball. The crucial difference is that not all of the balls are the same size or shape. They are also different densities. In some cases they can even combine to form larger balls, which then have a greater impact on any balls they run into. The impact that one ball or group of balls has on another might be so great that it destroys the ball. In this case the ratio of motion and rest that constituted the ball is disturbed such that the ball is no longer able to maintain its integrity. It becomes something else, several smaller balls perhaps. These smaller balls have their own ratio of motion and rest, which makes possible some affects but precludes others, and can thus enter into new combinations accordingly. The laws that govern these compositions and decompositions apply to any possible combination of bodies or groups of bodies.

At this point Spinoza makes an interesting claim that goes to the heart of what I have called his "experimentalism." Given that we are a ratio of motion and rest among our parts, Spinoza concludes that

> Whatever so disposes the human body that it can be affected in a great many ways, or renders it capable of affecting external bodies in a great many ways, is useful to man; the more it renders the body capable of being affected in a great many ways, or of affecting other bodies, the more useful it is; on the other hand, what renders the body less capable of these things is harmful.[5]

The more we are capable of interacting with the world, the better off we are. And, the less we are capable of interacting with the world, the worse off we are. Why does Spinoza come to this conclusion? For Spinoza the answer is simple. One can only be free to the degree that one understands and that understanding involves seeing the necessity of things. At the same time, we do not understand the necessity of things through "universals" by trying to think the "dog-ness" that accounts for all dogs. Rather, we only understand the necessity of things through their particularity by seeing how the ratio of motion and rest makes something capable of certain ways of affecting and being affected and seeing to what degree these affects are exercised. This type of knowledge cannot come from the misleading heights of the "universal" but can only come from the nitty-gritty engagement with individual bodies. It is only on the basis of this type of engagement that we can begin to see commonalities of properties across a wide range of objects. It is only then that we can see that a plow horse has more in common with an ox than a race horse.[6] The commonality is the result of similar affects and actually tells us something about what each animal can do, rather than a genetic and taxonomical claim that tells us nothing about what the animals can do. The kind of knowledge that Spinoza has in mind only comes through an engagement with the world. Thus, the more ways I can affect and be affected by the world, the more I can know, and the freer I will be. By the same token, whatever restricts my access to the world and prevents me from affecting and being affected leads to bondage.

While this is an interesting claim about knowledge, it seems to lead to insuperable ethical difficulties. By this point, it should come as no surprise that Spinoza is espousing something very different from what we normally call "ethics" or "morality." But, here he seems to come dangerously close to an ethical relativism in which each person decides what is right for him or herself. In fact Spinoza explicitly says, "By good I shall understand what we certainly know to be useful to us," and "By evil, however I shall understand what we certainly know prevents us from being masters of some good."[7] If the criterion by which I distinguish good and evil is whether or not it is useful to me, it is difficult to see how I could be consistent with myself, let alone consistent with other people. What is useful to me today may not be useful to me tomorrow. More seriously, my pursuit of what is useful to me right now may be an evil to you. Furthermore, if knowledge for Spinoza is so radically particularized, it looks like we could no more say that something is useful for all people at all times any more than we could say that something is useful for all dogs or all rocks at all times. Wouldn't it always depend on the particular affects that a particular person is capable of and the degree to which these affects are being exercised?

These are precisely the kind of questions that were raised in a series of letters between Spinoza and Willem van Blijenbergh. Although Blijenbergh initiates the correspondence in a congenial tone, the letters quickly turn into a sharp criticism of Spinoza's position particularly as regards the nature of ethics and the problem of evil. We'll focus on the ethical issues here. Blijenbergh poses the ethical question this way: "if there was a mind to whose singular nature the pursuit of sensual pleasure or knavery was not contrary, is there a reason for virtue which would have to move it to do good and omit evil?"[8] If it were useful to someone to act viciously, why wouldn't he or she do so? Spinoza's response to this question is terse and perhaps unexpected.

> Finally, your . . . question presupposes a contradiction. It is as if someone were to ask: if it agreed better with the nature of someone to hang himself, would there be reasons why he should not hang himself? But suppose it were possible that there should be such a nature. Then I say (whether I grant free will or not) that if anyone sees that he can live better on the gallows than at his table, he would act very foolishly if he did not go hang himself. One who saw clearly that in fact he would enjoy a better and more perfect life or essence by being a knave than by following virtue would also be a fool if he were not a knave. For acts of knavery would be virtue in relation to such a perverted human nature.[9]

On the one hand, Blijenbergh sees that Spinoza is only concerned with the particular individuals and accordingly asks about a singular nature whose ratio of motion and rest were constituted so that his ways affecting and being affected in the world were exercised such that he tended toward knavery. On the other hand, and this is where the contradiction lies, Blijenbergh wants to ask if a person so constituted would have a reason for not acting knavishly. For Spinoza this is tantamount to a tick having reason not to act like a tick. From Spinoza's perspective Blijenbergh is asking him to imagine the most farcical chimera, a dog with the affective traits of a fish, for example. If we could imagine a dog that swims better than it runs and can only breathe under water, of course it's better for such a dog to live under water. That's what's useful to it. If we could imagine a person (*per impossibile*) that would live better dead, then such a person should die as quickly as possible. Parlor games of this sort, however, completely miss the point.

Spinoza's reply, however, does more than point out the inherent contradiction in Blijenbergh's position. What is really at stake here is the possibility that being a knave might actually be useful to the knave. Spinoza denies this in the most strenuous terms, but not in terms that Blijenbergh finds compelling. The reason that Blijenbergh does not buy Spinoza's argument is that they're working with fundamentally different conceptions of virtue. Virtues for Blijenbergh are clearly prescriptive, they tell us what we ought to do, while for Spinoza, as we saw in the first chapter, virtues are descriptive, they tell us what is the case. This becomes explicit in Spinoza's definition of virtue in the *Ethics*, which Spinoza was working on at the same time as the Blijenbergh correspondence. "By virtue and power I understand the same thing, for example (by IIIP7), virtue, insofar as it is related to man, is the very essence, *or* nature, of man, insofar as he has the power of bringing about certain things, which can be understood through the laws of his nature alone."[10] Initially, this understanding of virtue seems to be at odds with Spinoza's concern with understanding things in their particularity rather than through a "universal." It seems as if Spinoza is providing here exactly the type of definition needed to give ethical prescriptions. But, a careful examination of Spinoza's claim shows that this is not the case. Virtue for Spinoza is nothing other than the ability to act in accordance with one's ratio of motion and rest. Those acts are virtuous that preserve this ratio, and those acts that disturb this ratio are vicious.

This explanation of virtue avoids the problem of Spinoza being inconsistent in his account of ethics in general, but at the same time it seems to repeat the definitions of "good" and "evil," which raised the specter of relativism. If virtue is nothing other than my ability to act in accordance with my nature, then this is saying that what is useful to me is good. The question then becomes, how do we avoid relativism given Spinoza's definition of good and his commitment to thinking things in their particularity? The answer lies in the careful wording of Spinoza's definition of "good" and "virtue." The key phrase in the definition of "good" is "what we certainly know," and the key phrase in the definition of "virtue" is "which can be understood through the laws of his nature alone." The implication of the definition of good is that we can be ignorant of what is good for us. If we understand ourselves or the world imperfectly, unclearly, then it is entirely possible that we can be mistaken about what is "good" for us. By the same token, certainly knowing what is good involves an understanding of things in their particularity and the necessary connection of their properties with other properties. Since we are finite, this kind of understanding lies on a continuum. Our knowledge can be more or less complete. The more complete our knowledge is, the more certainly do we know what is good for us.[11]

We could imagine a mushroom hunter as the perfect exemplar of Spinoza's position here. Mushroom hunting is necessarily slow and cautious, because the stakes are very high. One wrong choice might mean death. Additionally, mushroom hunting is very local. One cannot assume that all mushrooms that look like the edible mushrooms from one area will be equally edible. This highlights the great danger of forming "universals." The mushroom will interact with its environment in a unique way, which may very well entail the production of compounds toxic to humans. Only those mushrooms that "we certainly know" won't affect us adversely are "good."

Spinoza's discussion of "virtue" has similar parallels but also returns us to our discussion of bondage from the third chapter. When we act in accordance with our nature alone, we are virtuous. When our actions cannot be understood from our nature alone, we are vicious. In either case note that there is no ethical judgment being bestowed here. Spinoza is simply describing the necessary causal relation between acting in accord with one's nature, which tends toward the preservation of one's ratio of motion and rest, and combining with things that in certain respects are detrimental to one's ratio of motion and rest. I do not make an ethical *judgment* when I say, "Eating poison is unhealthy." I merely state the necessary causal relation between two opposed things combining and the effect that follows. When Spinoza says, "Hate can never be good," this is not a universal ethical judgment.[12] Rather, hate for Spinoza, as we saw in chapter 2, is a particular combination of ourselves with something that decreases our abilities, i.e., something that disagrees with our nature, disturbs our ratio of motion and rest. Hate functions exactly like poison and the results are predictably the same.

Thus, there are some ways of affecting and being affected that are in accord with our natures. This is the path of virtue. And, there are some ways of affecting and being affected that are opposed to our natures. This is the path of vice. The determining criterion here and the one that saves Spinoza from relativism is the role of the understanding. I can only walk the path of virtue to the degree that I understand the necessity of things. Insofar as I fail to understand the necessity of things I am bound to combine with things that are opposed to my nature. I am like a mushroom hunter who assumes that everything that looks like a Morel all over the world will be harmless. Such ignorance will undoubtedly tend toward the dissolution of my ratio of motion and rest rather than its preservation.

Now that we've seen in some respects the way that the human body interacts with its environment, we can look at how these interactions get played out on the different scales of religion, politics, and the environment. The terms will be the same; some interactions fortify bodies, while other interactions decompose bodies. Some interactions increase the ability of the human body to affect and be affected, while some interactions decrease the ability of the human body to affect and be affected. Some interactions increase understanding, while others decrease it. Spinoza will use this criterion as a way of distinguishing what is good and what is evil on these three scales.

NOTES

1. While we do not have time to explore this in detail, see Antonio Damasio's excellent analysis of Spinoza from the perspective of a neuroscientist, *Looking for Spinoza: Joy, Sorrow, and the Feeling Brain* (New York: Harcourt, Inc., 2003), 209ff.

2. IIL1.

3. IIPostulate1.

4. Deleuze, *Spinoza: Practical Philosophy*, 124–8.

5. IVP38.

6. See Deleuze, *Spinoza: Practical Philosophy*, 124.

7. IVD1 and D2.

8. Letter 22. All translations from Spinoza's correspondence are from *The Collected Works of Spinoza*, translated by Edwin Curley (Princeton: Princeton University Press, 1985). The Blijenbergh correspondence occurred over several months beginning in December 1664 through June 1665.

9. Letter 23.

10. IVD8.

11. The continuum of knowledge here is strictly parallel to the continuum of causality that ranges from inadequate to adequate. The more complete our knowledge is the more we are able to be the adequate cause of our actions.

12. IVP45.

Chapter 8
The Body Politic

Is it possible to walk into a room and gauge the "mood" of the room? Can we walk into a room and know that everyone is happy or sad? Does this happen only after we carefully observe, or do we simply "feel" it upon walking into the room? It has certainly often been my experience that I can walk into a room and know the mood of the room. I often have classes where I know immediately that the mood is buoyant, or flat. How exactly does this happen? Could it be that affect is transmitted more readily than we might like to believe? In addition, think about the possibility of a national mood. Can't the morale of a country be high or low? Aren't investors continually concerned with consumer confidence? Doesn't consumer confidence reinforce itself whether it's low or high, leading to depression (notice the affective term) on the low end or what Alan Greenspan called "irrational exuberance" (again an affective term) on the high end? These possibilities suggest that at least on some occasions we think of large, complex entities like countries as having affects and that these affects might be transmitted through the country as a whole.[1]

Spinoza capitalizes on this affective way of talking about politics. For Spinoza politics is essentially a problem in applied physics, a way of thinking about bodies in motion from a higher level of complexity. At the same time, politics is also essentially a problem in applied logic, a way of thinking about how ideas interact with other ideas. Of course, as we have seen, these two ways of talking about politics are simply two perspectives on a single entity. Both of these ways of pursuing politics are simply different ways of talking about complex individuals, first under the attribute of extension, second under the attribute of thought. The remarkable advantage that this gives Spinoza is that it allows him to talk about the way in which communities or countries affect and are affected. The difference between the way an individual person affects and is affected and the way a state affects and is affected is simply one of scale and complexity.

For Spinoza affects are transmitted among individuals the way that motion is transmitted among billiard balls. When we talk about very large and complex entities like states we need to make some qualifications. In the same way that a human body is very complex, because it is made up of numerous parts that are related to one another as a ratio of motion and rest, so is the state. The parts that the state is made up of, though, are human bodies as well as other organic and inorganic components. So, in the state we have a very complex entity that is itself made up of very complex entities. What follows from complexity for Spinoza is the ability to affect and be affected. The more complex an individual is, the more ways it can affect and be affected. Thus, if a human can affect and be affected in ways too many to count, a state's ways of affecting and being affected would be exponentially greater. At the same time, the ways of defining a state would mirror the way that we defined a tick in the previous chapter. A state's ways of affecting and being affected would provide a latitudinal coordinate, and the degree to which it exercises those affects would provide a longitudinal coordinate. Thus, concerning a state (or any group of people for that matter) one would not ask the "universal" question, What kind of state is it? One would ask what the state is capable of. The answers that one would give to this question could not be too subtle and would depend on an enormous range of factors: demographics, past history, economics, international relations, governing structure, geography, geology, education, technology, religion, etc. All of these would serve to define what a state is capable of. Thus, for example, a state whose agricultural technology was limited would only be able to produce food for a limited number of people. Such a state could only support a larger population through trade or conquest. Another state might have very advanced agricultural technology but be limited in its use by geography. A third state, in order to consolidate its internal power, might limit its contacts with other states. Such a move would increase the control it has over its own citizens but limit the possibility of expanding its territories.[2]

Since for Spinoza the difference between a human body and a body politic is simply one of scale and complexity, let's build the state from the ground up in Spinoza's terms. As we've seen in previous chapters, since everything is part of the same universe, any part can combine with any other part. At the same time, however, any combination of parts may enhance, destroy, or remain indifferent to the parts that enter into the combination. Thus, my combination with good food enhances me, my combination with poison destroys me, and my combination with the dust on the keyboard has no effect on me. The principle that dominates Spinoza's ethics is to seek out those combinations that enhance me rather than those that destroy me. Up to this point, we've mostly been concerned with the way in which I combine detrimentally with other people and objects. But the key to beneficial combinations lies in understanding what is useful to us. In this light Spinoza claims that many things are useful to us, but that the most useful thing conceivable is another person who fully agrees with our nature. When combined with such a person my ability to affect and be affected is doubled. I am twice as powerful as I was prior to the combination. The difficulty here is finding someone who fully agrees with my nature. Does this mean I must find someone exactly like me? Unless I have a twin somewhere that I'm unaware of, this seems unlikely. For Spinoza there can only be one way in which someone agrees with my nature and I with his or her nature, that is, through understanding. I can't even agree with myself unless I understand the necessity of things. Thus, the only way to agree in nature with anyone else is if both of us understand the necessity of things. Or, to put this another way, people can only agree in their virtue. They cannot agree in their vice. To the degree that people are vicious, they are toxic to their neighbors.

The ideal state for Spinoza, then, is one in which no one wishes anything for himself that he does not also wish for his neighbor, and where each person consents to form a community based on understanding the necessity of things. Several things need to be noted about Spinoza's ideal state. First, note that Spinoza is a social contract theorist. This means that a political community can only be formed by the consent of the governed. Spinoza is in the vanguard of the social contract movement, which has its origins in Hobbes (whom Spinoza read) and progresses through Locke (the most influential form in the founding of America) and culminates in perhaps the best known theorist of the social contract, Rousseau (who was hugely influential on later theorists like Kant and Hegel, both positively and negatively). What social contract theorists all have in common is that civil society works like a contract. We all enter into a bargain when we live in a society. The bargain usually works something like this: we give up some of the rights that we naturally possess in exchange for a new set of rights granted to us by the government we form. In return the government defends this new set of rights in us.

For most social contract theorists the moment of consent divides history into two parts: the state of nature, which precedes consent, and civil society, which follows consent. Different social contract theorists look at the state of nature in wildly divergent ways. Hobbes, for example, famously said that life in the state of nature was "solitary, poor, nasty, brutish, and short." Rousseau, on the other hand, thought that the state of nature was a glorious paradise where we were free from the chains of society. It is Rousseau's conception of the state of nature that gives us "the noble savage." Locke falls somewhere in the middle of these two extremes. In addition, it's not entirely clear whether any of these thinkers thought the state of nature actually existed. What is clear, though, is that each posits it as a way of contrasting what we naturally are with our position vis-á-vis society.

In contrast to these better known social contract theorists, Spinoza does not seem to have a conception of the state of nature. The reason for this is that he has a different conception of right than these other thinkers. All of these other thinkers depend on a "universal" conception of human nature in which rights inhere. Since Spinoza avoids thinking about human nature in this way, he is not forced into this kind of thought experiment. On Spinoza's model "rights" are exactly equivalent to what I'm capable of. Rights are nothing other than my ways of affecting and being affected, which is made possible by my ratio of motion and rest. Thus, rights are not some additional property that follows from a "universal" essence, but simply another way of talking about my power or virtue. I can enter into relations that increase or decrease my power, but these are not fundamentally related to whether I'm the citizen of a state. It is true that for Spinoza being a member of a state can make me much more powerful than I would be alone, but this shift in power cannot be explained in terms of a traditional discourse of rights. The shift in power comes from the new combinations that I'm able to enter into as a result of being a citizen of a state.

Another crucial difference aims squarely at Hobbes, the only social contract theorist Spinoza could have been familiar with. For Hobbes, the only reason that one would enter into the social contract is fear. Out of fear for my life, I give all my rights to a sovereign who rules absolutely. Fear for Spinoza is a sad passion connected to the idea of a future external cause. As a sad passion it indicates a reduction in my power. A state predicated on fear, by Spinoza's lights, would be very weak indeed. No one could be himself in Hobbes's state, except for perhaps the sovereign. In contrast to this, Spinoza proposes that the state be predicated on understanding. It's only to the degree that we understand ourselves and our world that we can seek out what is truly useful, rather than what our fear drives us to. Furthermore, it is only in such a state that we can be ourselves, that we can affect and be affected in the most possible ways. Such a state does not foreclose on possible combinations, as a Hobbesian state would. Such a state increases the number and type of combinations that we might enter into.

In his unfinished *Political Treatise* Spinoza discusses the problem of being ruled by fear. He writes that "a state that looks only to govern by fear will be one free from vice rather than endowed with virtue."[3] His point is that it is possible to make people do the right thing through fear. The problem is that in such a case the citizens do the right thing for the wrong reason. Their motivation does not follow from their own nature but from the fear of the government. In contrast to this Spinoza says, "Men should be governed in such a way that they do not think of themselves as being governed but as living as they please . . . so that their only restraint is love of freedom."[4] If all act in one accord and seek only that which understanding suggests, the state will not be opposed to the people but the combination of all their powers.

The real danger to the state from the perspective of its citizens appears in the form of an affect that overwhelms all good sense. Here Spinoza returns to the principles he carefully lays out in the *Ethics*.

> But an objection can still be raised as follows, that although the constitutions set forth above may have the support of reason and the common sentiment of men, there are times when they can nevertheless be overthrown, for there is no emotion that is not sometimes overpowered by a stronger contrary emotion.[5]

Here Spinoza echoes the proposition from *Ethics* IVP7, which makes clear that there are only ways of affecting and being affected, and that affects cannot be done away with, only replaced. If the affect is strong enough it can replace the current affect. This is as true of states as it is of people. Spinoza continues,

> So however well a commonwealth is organized and however good its constitution, yet when the state is in the grip of some crisis and everyone, as commonly happens, is seized with a kind of panic, they all pursue a course prompted only by their immediate fears with no regard for the future or the laws; all turn to the man who is renowned for his victories, they set him free from the laws, they extend his command—a very bad precedent—and entrust the entire commonwealth to his good faith.[6]

Reading this quote, it is difficult not to think about what happened in America following the terrorist attacks of September 11, 2001. In many instances the rule of law was suspended and the executive branch was given unprecedented powers to respond to this attack. To the degree, though, that we responded out of fear rather than through understanding, we have damaged ourselves. We have restricted the number and kind of combinations that we can enter into. We have not been ourselves as a country; that is, we have disturbed the ratio of motion and rest that constitutes the state and are currently heading as a country down the path of foolishness rather than wisdom. This has been painfully obvious on the international stage as other states and NGOs ask us to return to the rule of law that has won us the admiration and jealousy of the rest of the world. Perhaps the next administration can help rectify this.

As I write this the U.S. financial markets are imploding. The mortgage crisis has either bankrupt or crippled all of the investment banks in the country. The stock markets have responded to this crisis by a precipitous reduction in value. (On Spinoza's view the stock market would be nothing but a register of affects.) The proposed solution to this problem is to grant the Secretary of the Treasury, Henry M. Paulson, unlimited power and no accountability in the spending of $700 billion to bail out these financial institutions. The same basic mechanism is at work here. When crisis leads to panic, we immediately rush to follow our fears in the hopes of quelling them as quickly as possible. Unfortunately, though, when we follow our fears, whether as an individual or as a state, we are not being ourselves. We remain at the mercy of the external cause, rather than doing what is truly useful to us. The result is always a diminution of our power to affect and be affected. We cannot act according to our fear and be free at the same time.

If Spinoza has made it sufficiently clear that a state led by fear is not free, it is still not entirely clear what he supposes the state might do. Here again, the same rules apply to the state as they do the individual. States seek to persevere in their existence, and as with anything, states can only maintain their existence by acting in accordance with their nature. The nature of a state is to be made up of individuals with certain properties. If the state prevents some of these individuals from acting according to their nature, this is equivalent to a person putting on a blindfold. In such a case part of the person is not allowed to act according to its nature. As a result, the body's power to act is diminished. By the same token a state that represses part of itself will reduce its power to act. Spinoza's concern, then, is the proper functioning of the state, which entails each of its parts acting in agreement with one another. The tricky thing for Spinoza, though, is how one avoids a kind of totalitarianism where everyone walks in lockstep with the wishes of the government. The key is governing in such a way that people are allowed to be themselves rather than reacting to the rule of the state. Spinoza in his *Theological-Political Treatise* writes,

> It is not, I repeat, the purpose of the state to transform men from rational beings into beasts or puppets, but rather to enable them to develop their mental and physical faculties in safety, to use their reason without restraint and to refrain from the strife and the vicious mutual abuse that are prompted by hatred, anger or deceit. Thus the purpose of the state is, in reality, freedom.[7]

While it might be possible for the state to preserve itself for a time by turning its citizens into puppets, ultimately such a state would destroy itself. The state would destroy itself because it is acting in opposition to the parts that make it up.

For Spinoza the purpose of the state, freedom, is achieved through the freedom of speech. Spinoza takes it as impossible that any government could control the thoughts of its citizens. Thus, the only question remaining is whether the state would best preserve itself by controlling the speech of its members. In response to this Spinoza offers the following *reductio ad absurdum*: If a state were able to control speech to such a degree that only speech favored by the state could be uttered, the result would be that people would be saying one thing while thinking another. The consequences of this for the state would be disastrous. In the first place it would undermine any trust that the citizenry would have in one another. No one would know if a speaker really meant what she said, or if she was saying what was required of her by the state. At the same time "the disgusting arts of sycophancy and treachery would be encouraged." Finally, speech itself would be impoverished. Certain combinations of words would be outlawed. No one would invent new combinations of words for fear that they might be interpreted as seditious. Not only would all forms of poetry, literature, and drama cease, but public discourse, where it had not dried up all together, would take the form of officially sanctioned rote formulas. It's almost as if Spinoza had read George Orwell's *1984*.

Even more seriously, Spinoza thinks revolution would follow closely on such measures. He doesn't think it's possible that people would only say what the law required of them. Or at least, such a law would hamper the best in the state while encouraging the worst. Furthermore, those hampered by the law would begin to resent it, their resentment being "most aroused when beliefs which they think to be true are treated as criminal. . . . In consequence, they are emboldened to denounce the laws and go to all lengths to oppose the magistrate, considering it not a disgrace but honorable to stir up sedition and to resort to any outrageous action in this cause."[8] The strange paradox of outlawing freedom of speech is that it punishes the honest and rewards the obsequious. It forces people of good will to behave like criminals, and the criminals profit from this restriction of speech, since they can enrich themselves by denouncing anyone they choose as proclaiming and fomenting traitorous speech.

Those who persist in denying freedom of speech would argue that too much is at stake to let people speak freely. Free speech is how heresies and half-truths predominate. Surely these lead more quickly to the state's ruin than repressed speech. Spinoza's response to this objection is twofold. First, if the state legislates the truth, it immediately divides its citizenry into oppressors and oppressed. The oppressed will feel themselves persecuted and be more likely to turn against the state, while the oppressors will feel themselves uniquely privileged in the state. And, of course, a privilege granted is not easily rescinded, so any change of heart on the government's part would risk alienating the other group and fomenting rebellion. Second, if the government solves debates by legislation, every opposing group will seek to have its views codified into law. This will create warring factions both within the government and in the public as each group seeks to have its views enforced on the rest of the citizenry. The resulting political campaigns would be unrelated to the truth as each side, already convinced of the rightness of its cause, would seek to sway the political process by any means necessary. If, on the other hand, the government refused to settle such debates by legislation they wouldn't escalate politically and disturb the peace of the state.

Based on these analyses Spinoza summarizes his conclusions: 1) It is impossible to deny people the freedom to say what they think. Thus, any attempt to deny it will result in a state divided against itself. 2) Freedom of speech can be given to everyone without endangering the authority of the state. The state always maintains its ability to restrict how people act and in this way maintains the security of its citizens. 3) Everyone can speak freely without endangering the public peace. This does not deny that some speeches themselves can cause riots, but that the authority of the state should lie in quelling the riot, not free speech. 4) Free speech does not endanger piety. Obviously, the great concern of Spinoza's time was the doctrinal disputes among various Protestant groups and with Roman Catholicism. Speaking freely about these doctrines and pursuing honest debate about them doesn't endanger piety but strengthens it. 5) Most importantly, not only does the freedom to say what one thinks not endanger the state, public peace, or piety, but it actually preserves them. Spinoza has shown time and again that even though it seems that restricting speech would maintain the state and its peace, ultimately it subverts them.[9]

For Spinoza, then, the most crucial thing that the state can preserve is the freedom of speech. The citizens depend on it as a means to pursuing the greatest number of ways of affecting and being affected, which in turn makes the state capable of a greater number of affections. The type of government most likely to bring about such a state is a democratic one. Spinoza writes,

> Therefore, if honesty is to be prized rather than obsequiousness, and if sovereigns are to retain full control and not be forced to surrender to agitators, it is imperative to grant freedom of judgment and to govern men in such a way that the different and conflicting views they openly proclaim do not debar them from living together in peace. This system of government is undoubtedly the best and its disadvantages are fewer because it is in closest accord with human nature. For we have shown that in a democracy (which comes closest to the natural state) all the citizens undertake to act, but not to reason and to judge, by decision made in common. That is to say, since all men cannot think alike, they agree that a proposal supported by a majority of votes shall have the force of a decree, meanwhile retaining the authority to repeal the same when they see a better alternative. Thus the less freedom of judgment is conceded to men, the further their distance from the most natural state, and consequently the more oppressive the regime.[10]

For Spinoza the way to solve a political problem is identical to the way to solve an ethical problem. The most important issue is identifying the way in which all of the constituent parts are related to one another. Only then can we understand what such an individual is capable of. The only difference between a person and a state at this level of analysis is one of scale. Once we understand an individual's ratio of motion and rest and its ways of affecting and being affected, two paths naturally appear, the path of wisdom and the path of foolishness. Acting in accord with an individual's nature (whether person or state) tends toward its preservation, while acting in opposition to it tends away from its preservation. Spinoza's claim is that the path on which a state tends toward its preservation is democracy, because this is the path that understands that a crucial component of any state is people, and it is only to the degree that people are able to think what they like and say what they think that this crucial component is preserved.

NOTES

1. See Teresa Brennan's profoundly Spinozist account of this phenomenon in *The Transmission of Affect* (Ithaca, N.Y.: Cornell University Press, 2004).

2. Manuel DeLanda in *A Thousand Years of Nonlinear History* (New York: Zone Publishing, 1997) and *A New Philosophy of Society: Assemblage Theory and Social Complexity* (New York: Continuum, 2006), does a remarkable job of showing how different kinds of communities form depending on the way in which each is able to capture and manipulate flows of matter-energy.

3. All references to *The Political Treatise* from Samuel Shirley's translation in *Spinoza: Complete Works* (Indianapolis: Hackett Publishing, 2002). The references refer to the book number in Roman numerals followed by the chapter number. The designator TP

distinguishes this work from the *Theological-Political Treatise*, which is abbreviated TTP. Thus, the above quote is cited, TP X:8.

4. TP X:8.
5. TP X:10.
6. TP X:10.
7. All references to the *Theological-Political Treatise* are also from Shirley's translation in *Spinoza: Complete Works* (Indianapolis: Hackett Publishing, 2002). The *Treatise* is abbreviated TTP, followed by the chapter number, then the page number to the Shirley translation is given. Thus, the above quote would be TTP 20/567.
8. TTP 20/569.
9. TTP 20/571–2.
10. TTP 20/571.

Chapter 9
Religion

For Spinoza religion and politics are inseparable. This is not to say that the state should legislate in religious matters, which we saw in the previous chapter. Religion for Spinoza is another way that groups of people can affect and be affected. As a result, it is properly thought along the same lines as politics. The same process of definition in terms of affect and the degree to which those affects are exercised is still operative. Furthermore, the criterion by which a religion can be evaluated is the same, too. Does the religion increase the number of ways of affecting and being affected (i.e., is it useful?), or does it decrease the affections (i.e., is it harmful?). It is precisely because religion and politics are so closely related that Spinoza devotes one of his major published works to both, the *Theological-Political Treatise*. The topic also arises in some of his correspondence, particularly his exchange with Blijenbergh. As both of these works make clear, as well as the *Ethics*, the first section of which is simply entitled "God," Spinoza's understanding of God and religion are far from orthodox. What I'd like to do in this chapter is explore Spinoza's account of some basic theological concepts and how these affect his claims about religion.

One of the Christian theological debates that raged in Holland during Spinoza's lifetime concerned the sovereignty of God. For some the sovereignty of God entailed that sinners and saints were predestined from all eternity. To suggest that God could provide the means of salvation without anyone necessarily being saved is an affront to God's absolute control over the universe. The other side would argue that God's love demands that people be free to choose their path, and thus love or hate God freely in return. The difference between these two sides is often characterized as two kinds of bridges. In the first instance, those affirming God's sovereignty to the utmost would argue that, although the bridge that spans the gulf between God and humanity is narrow, it necessarily covers the full distance. In the second instance, those affirming God's love have a very wide bridge, but there is nothing that guarantees that the bridge will span the gulf.

Let's take the poles of sovereignty and love as starting points for understanding Spinoza's position. The traditional facets of God's sovereignty are omniscience (God knows all.), omnipotence (God is all-powerful.), and omnipresence (God is everywhere.). Spinoza would argue that each of these facets necessarily belongs to God. God for Spinoza is omniscient, omnipotent, and omnipresent. The catch for Spinoza, as far as traditional theology is concerned, is that in order to affirm these properties one must conceive of God in a radically heterodox way. One must dissolve the traditional creator/created distinction that undergirds the major monotheistic religions: Islam, Judaism, and Christianity.

For Spinoza dissolving this presupposition is in fact the only way to maintain the predicates of omniscience, omnipotence, and omnipresence, the only way to maintain God's sovereignty. The simple reason is this: In order for God to know all or possess all power or be everywhere, God would have to be infinite, which in Spinoza's terms would mean that God cannot be limited by anything else. This, of course, is identical to claiming that God is substance, which had been the dominant way of conceiving God for the previous millennia and a half. So far, Spinoza is on board with this. God is infinite, and God is substance. The hitch occurs when traditional theologies make their next move; namely, God is separate from creation. God transcends the universe. For Spinoza this cannot follow. Infinity and transcendence are mutually exclusive terms. Initially this seems like an odd claim as we have become so accustomed to thinking infinity and transcendence as complementary, as if they mutually implied one another. Spinoza explicitly denies this mutual implication, though. Transcendence implies a relation between two things, the transcendent and the transcended. But, if there are two things regardless of their relation, then they necessarily limit one another. If they limit one another, then neither thing can be infinite. And, if neither thing is infinite, then God cannot be omniscient, omnipotent, or omnipresent. Thus, Spinoza salvages infinity by denying transcendence.

By denying transcendence Spinoza abandons all hope of being considered orthodox by his contemporaries. His views made him infamous throughout Europe both during and after his lifetime. As we saw briefly above, Spinoza's position is a pantheism that makes God and the universe identical. Throughout the *Ethics* Spinoza's constant refrain is "God or nature" (*Deus sive natura*). These terms are equivalent in every way for Spinoza and completely interchangeable. Although this position caused Spinoza a great deal of religious and political trouble, from a purely philosophical standpoint his solution is quite elegant. Is God sovereign for Spinoza? Absolutely. Because there is nothing other than God. Everything is part of God, therefore everything follows necessarily from the divine nature. Is God omniscient for Spinoza? Certainly, all knowledge is contained in God. There is no knowledge that can be conceived other than God's knowledge. In our knowing of the universe we merely think finitely what God thinks infinitely. Is God omnipotent for Spinoza? Unquestionably. As God is simply another way of talking about nature as a whole, the big picture, God necessarily contains all power. No power can be conceived other than God's power. Finally, omnipresence is a cinch. God is present everywhere, because God is identical to every "where." There is no "where" that God does not exist.

Now that we see how Spinoza maintains God's sovereignty we can turn to the other pole of the debate, God's love. Spinoza's position here, which follows from his pantheism, in many ways moves him even farther away from traditional monotheistic conceptions of God. "Strictly speaking, God loves no one, and hates no one."[1] Christianity in particular is wont to see the whole drama of creation, fall, and redemption as motivated by God's love of humanity. But, Spinoza takes this to be the most egregious kind of anthropomorphism. To see why that is, let's think about Spinoza's definition of "love." It is an increase in perfection accompanied by the idea of an external cause. From Spinoza's perspective there are two profound problems with attributing love to God. First, God is infinitely perfect and so can undergo no increase or decrease in perfection. Or, to state this even more succinctly, "God is without passions."[2] Second, the idea of an external cause is incoherent in relation to God. There is nothing external to God, so God cannot be affected by an external cause.

If God cannot, in principle, love us, what about our relation to God or God's self-relation? Here things get a little trickier. We can love God, even though we cannot expect God to love us in return. What exactly, though, does our love of God consist in? For Spinoza, the love of God brings us back to the "intuitive knowledge" or the "third kind of knowledge" that we examined in the fifth chapter. As we saw, the third kind of knowledge understands the way in which everything follows necessarily from the laws of the universe. And as we now know, we can replace the phrase "laws of the universe" with "God." Thus, on Spinoza's account the third kind of knowledge is nothing other than the knowledge of God as the necessary cause of all things. It is precisely in this third kind of knowledge that we find what Spinoza calls the "intellectual love of God." This is still love in the same sense that we just examined. The crucial difference is that the object that is the source of joy here is God, the big picture, not some particular object. The intellectual love of God is nothing other than understanding the necessity of things from the perspective of the whole, under the aspect of eternity (*sub specie aeternitatis*).

The more vexing issue is God's self-relation. On this score Spinoza says, "God loves himself with an infinite intellectual love."[3] So far so good, God enjoys infinite perfection and takes himself to be the cause of it. This is God's love of self. In the next proposition, though, things get strange.

> The mind's intellectual love of God is the very love of God by which God loves himself, not insofar as he is infinite, but insofar as he can be explained by the human mind's essence, considered under a species of eternity; i.e., the mind's intellectual love of God is part of the infinite love by which God loves himself.[4]

In this proposition Spinoza makes a distinction between God's self-love in terms of God's infinity and in terms of the human mind's ability to understand. On the one hand, this is still part of the way that God loves himself but from the perspective of a finite human mind.

The corollary to this proposition, though, seems to flatly contradict Spinoza's earlier statements. "From this it follows that insofar as God loves himself, he loves men, and consequently that God's love of men and the mind's intellectual love of God are one and the same."[5] God's love of self is not a passion but follows from God's nature. God's love of self is necessarily the love of everything, since God and everything are identical. When we understand things from the third kind of knowledge, we see the necessity of all things and therefore find nothing worthy of hatred. So, for Spinoza God loves people through the understanding of other people. Notice his language in the note to this proposition:

> From this we clearly understand wherein our salvation, *or* blessedness, *or* freedom, consists, viz. in a constant and eternal love of God, or in God's love of men. And this love, or blessedness, is called glory in the Sacred Scriptures—not without reason. For whether this love is related to God or to the mind, it can rightly be called satisfaction of mind, which is really not distinguished from glory. For insofar as it is related to God it is joy . . . , accompanied by the idea of himself. And similarly insofar as it is related to the mind.[6]

Spinoza completely reinscribes the language of salvation within his account of God and freedom. Here we see Spinoza's general strategy with regard to past traditions, whether philosophical, political, or religious. He appropriates their most important terms—substance, ethics, right, salvation, etc.,—and shows that when they are thought rigorously an entirely new system arises. Thus, in the same way that substance becomes pantheism, and ethics and right become ways of describing affects, so salvation becomes a new way of seeing the world as an interconnected and necessary whole. Salvation, then, is not the result of a *judgment* delivered by God or humanity or a book, but the necessary consequence of seeing the world in a particular way. For Spinoza, we are "saved" to the degree that we understand that things could not be otherwise. Any other way of understanding salvation will result in being chained to external causes that are opposed to our nature.

Traditionally, salvation is connected to notions of an immortal soul. What gets saved, then, is my soul, which is usually opposed to my body. Spinoza does have a conception of immortality, or more precisely eternality, but as we saw above it cannot involve any kind of dualism. What exactly could be eternal about modes that coagulate temporarily under a ratio of motion and rest? Clearly, the ratio of motion and rest among the parts of a body cannot be maintained forever. At the same time, Spinoza is quite clear that one's thoughts can be more and more occupied with the necessity of things, that is, the ordering of one's thoughts with God as the cause. God, though, is eternal, and to order one's thoughts with God as the cause is to think things from the perspective of eternity (*sub specie aeternitatis*). To the degree that we think things from the perspective of eternity we are eternal. Spinoza puts it this way, "He who has a body capable of a great many things has a mind whose greatest part is eternal."[7] A capable body, one that acts rather than being passive, is at the same time (seen under the attribute of thought) a mind that is mostly eternal.

From the top, then, here is Spinoza's salvation narrative. Vice, sin, and bondage are the result of being controlled by external causes opposed to my nature. Virtue, salvation, and freedom depend on my acting in accordance with my nature, preserving myself. This preservation can only occur to the degree that I understand all things as following necessarily from God's nature. To the degree that I do this I am virtuous; I am free; I act; I am saved. All of these are synonymous, for Spinoza, with being eternal. If I act, it is only to the degree that I understand, and understanding is understanding from the perspective of eternity.

Anyone can readily see that Spinoza's salvation narrative sets him in stark opposition to the major monotheistic religions. Even though he quotes the Bible approvingly, his views on the whole do not seem in accord with the Bible. In his correspondence with Blijenbergh, when Blijenbergh claims that the two rules by which he philosophizes are "clear and distinct conceptions of [his] intellect and the revealed word, or will, of God,"[8] Spinoza responds in his characteristically frank manner that, "I do not understand Sacred Scripture, though, I have spent several years on it. . . . So I am completely satisfied with what the intellect shows me. . . . For truth does not contradict the truth."[9]

In Spinoza's response there are several underlying principles at work that he explicates more fully in the *Theological-Political Treatise*. The first of these principles is that the Bible is an historical document produced over a long period of time and reflects this history in numerous ways. Since each of the various authors sought to speak to his own time, the method and content of this speaking is appropriate to the time. Spinoza is adamant, though, that what is appropriate to one age may not accomplish the same purpose in a different age. This counsels caution when reading any part of the Bible. The second principle, and this follows from the first, is that the purpose of the Bible or any of its parts is not to reveal deep metaphysical mysteries. The Bible is a guide to piety, not a philosophical text. To treat the Bible as a philosophical text is to misunderstand its purpose and to be led into error. The position that Spinoza takes up here is known as "accommodationism," which holds that whatever is written in the Bible is written for a specific time and place and that one cannot assume that all scripture applies to all times and all places. He was one of the first to take up this position and argue for it on the basis of the history and construction of the biblical text. In doing this he was a forerunner of the historical-critical method that has dominated biblical studies since the nineteenth century. Spinoza's accommodationism leads him to distinguish between the historical text of the Bible and the word of God. The word of God is that in the Bible that leads us to piety. Thus, while the text of the Bible can be corrupted, the word of God cannot.

What is revealed of the word of God in the Bible for Spinoza is very simple and straightforward,

> for this leads obviously to the conclusion that Scripture demands nothing from men but obedience, and condemns not ignorance but obstinacy. Furthermore, since obedience to God consists in loving one's neighbor, it follows that Scripture commands no other kind of knowledge than that which is necessary for all men before they can obey God according to this commandment, and without which men are bound to be self-willed, or at least unschooled to obedience. Other philosophic questions which do not directly tend to this end, whether they are concerned with knowledge of God or with knowledge of nature, have nothing to do with Scripture, and should therefore be dissociated from revealed religion.[10]

Of course, as we saw above, Spinoza has a singular vision of what it means to love God and one's neighbor. Both of these are the result of seeing the necessity of all things, or knowing by the third kind of knowledge. This is precisely why Spinoza makes the distinction that he does between the Bible and the word of God, which results in the distinction between obedience and knowledge in the previous quote. One cannot know the necessary relation among substance, attributes, and modes from the Bible, but one can learn obedience to a few basic rules of conduct. This is the Bible's only task and the only extent to which it contains the word of God. Any other use is a misuse.

While the simplicity of Spinoza's account has much that is appealing about it, some might argue that it has the disadvantage of making much of the Bible superfluous. Everything that does not deal with loving God or neighbor could be removed without damaging the fundamental message and purpose of the various texts. Chief among the things that would be removed are the miracles, insofar as miracles are defined as abrogations of the laws of nature. As we have seen the laws of nature and God's laws are identical and cannot be contravened. For Spinoza a miracle would entail God acting in opposition to his nature, which is inconceivable. Or, to put it another way, it would involve conceiving of God having a will that could act in opposition to his nature, another absurdity. The biggest problem that arises at this point, at least for Christianity, is the resurrection of Christ. His death and resurrection is the cornerstone of Christian belief. Paul says that without the resurrection faith in Christ is in vain.[11] But for Spinoza the resurrection would be a miracle that asks us to believe that God can act in opposition to his nature. What then is the purpose of resurrection? Spinoza would say that like all accounts of miracles in the Bible they serve the purpose of leading us to piety. They teach us to walk obediently in the love of God and the love of one's neighbor.

Spinoza's account of the purpose of the Bible brings us to the practice of religion. Spinoza has deep and abiding concerns about the way religion has been historically practiced. His chief concern is the role that superstition plays in the control that religion has over people's lives. Superstition arises, according to Spinoza, because when we are unable to control our lives, for example when tragedy strikes, we immediately begin searching for something to reassert that control. In this state we will believe *anything* in the hopes of reasserting our mastery over our lives. The source of superstition thus lies in fear, fear of the unknown, fear of never regaining control. Because the source of superstition lies in fear, and since fear is "an inconstant sadness, which has . . . arisen from the image of a doubtful thing" everyone is subject to superstition.[12] Or, superstition is a constant danger because we don't know the future. Now the types of superstition that can arise are as varied and multiple as the external causes that give rise to fear in the first place. Spinoza's concern, though, is when these superstitions become institutionalized, sustained and repeated through a large number of people over a long period of time. In order for this to happen, the superstition has to be nurtured and tended. This occurs through affects that support and magnify the superstition: "hope, hatred, anger, and deceit."[13] It is easy to see why hatred, anger, and deceit would sustain superstition. Anger and hatred, in particular, thrive on imagining that things could have been otherwise, which redoubles one's efforts to maintain superstitious practices in order to prevent a tragedy from repeating itself. Deceit is also straightforward. If I am deceived about what my future holds or the causes of my misfortune, then I will certainly misunderstand the solution to my problems and fall into superstition. Hope, though, seems oddly out of place. Isn't hope that which dispels fear, allows us to face the future boldly? How could hope sustain superstition? The key to answering these questions lies in the nature of hope itself. Spinoza defines hope as "nothing but an inconstant joy which has arisen from the image of a future or past thing whose outcome we doubt."[14] Notice the parallel between hope and fear here. In one sense they are opposed, since one results in joy and the other sadness. But, this should not obscure the fact that structurally they are identical; both arise out of inconstancy, and both are dependent on external causes. The way, then, that hope might support superstition, is through the hope that acting in accord with the superstition will change one's lot.

Spinoza's account of religion seeks to remove superstition as the impetus for its practice. This attempt to remove superstition is two-pronged. First, show what true religion is, and at the same time expose the errors of false religion. Second, show what true salvation consists in. What Spinoza wants to avoid above all is having people motivated by either fear or hope, which as we saw above is his goal with regard to politics. If I love God or my neighbor out of the fear of God's judgment, or if I do these things out of hope for some future reward, then I have failed to love both God and neighbor. My motivation in both cases cannot be love, but is in fact that inconstant object that produces sadness or joy in me. These are more instances when I am not myself, where my actions are determined by something other than my nature. In such a case I am not free but in bondage. To do the right thing out of fear of punishment or hope of reward is not to do the right thing at all but to be controlled by superstition. Spinoza is quite blunt about those who are moral or pious from superstition.

> For most people apparently believe that they are free to the extent that they are permitted to yield to their lust, and that they give up their right to the extent that they are bound to live according to the rule of the divine law. Morality, then, and religion, and absolutely everything related to strength of character [virtue], they believe to be burdens, which they hope to put down after death, when they also hope to receive a reward for their "bondage," that is, for their morality and religion. They are induced to live according to the rule of the divine law (as far as their weakness and lack of character allows) not only by this hope, but also, and especially, by the fear that they may be punished horribly after death. If men did not have this hope and fear [they say], but believed instead that minds die with the body, and that the wretched, exhausted with the burden of morality, cannot look forward to a life to come, they would return to their natural disposition and would prefer to govern all their actions according to lust, and to obey fortune rather than themselves.[15]

The argument for superstition is deceptively powerful and long-lived. If hope and fear are not held over people and used to coerce them into piety and morality, society itself will break down. People will become bestial, living only according to their lusts. So, for the good of all, the keepers of superstition argue, we must maintain people in their superstition by whatever means necessary. It's for their own good. The corollary to this is that piety and morality are themselves seen as burdensome, rather than descriptive of living well.

For Spinoza everything related to virtue is its own reward, including piety and morality. His reply to the above argument is devastating.

> These opinions seem no less absurd to me than if someone, because he does not believe he can nourish his body with good food to eternity, should prefer to fill himself with poisons and other deadly things, or because he sees that the mind is not eternal, or immortal, should prefer to be mindless, and to live without reason. These [common beliefs] are so absurd they are hardly worth mentioning.[16]

It is so much more preferable and beneficial to have people pursuing religion and morality because these represent the codification and institutionalization of what is useful for preserving our existence. To do so for any other reason is bondage, and those who argue that our bondage is a safeguard against a worse bondage fail to understand the nature of the problem.

In an era of increasing religious intolerance and political unrest, Spinoza argues that peace can only be found through freedom. Freedom in the political sense means the freedom to say what one thinks. Freedom in the religious sense means freedom from superstition and its source in fear and its supports in hope, hatred, anger, and despair. Both religious and political freedom depend on the true freedom that comes through understanding God, the world, and oneself according to the intuitive knowledge that sees the necessary connection of all things.

NOTES

1. VP17C.
2. VP17.
3. VP35.
4. VP36.
5. VP36C.
6. VP36S.
7. VP39.
8. Letter 20.
9. Letter 21.
10. TTP 13/510–11.
11. 1 Corinthians 15:14.
12. IIIP18S2.
13. TTP Preface/389.
14. IIIP18S2.
15. VP41S.
16. VP41S.

Chapter 10
The Environment

In *The Simpsons* episode "The Old Man and the Lisa" an early scene illustrates what is at stake in our relation to the environment. Mr. Burns has come to Springfield Elementary to talk to the students participating in the Junior Achievers Club. The club, like its real-life counterpart, is designed to foster the values of hard work and capitalism. Mr. Burns, as the town's richest man, is a likely person to give advice to such a group. However, Lisa, ever the agitator for social justice, begins to press Mr. Burns on his nuclear plant's relation to the environment, asking if there is a recycling program. As Mr. Burns sounds out the word, he comes to the realization that he's never heard of the word. Lisa explains that recycling is one of the ways that we help Mother Nature. Mr. Burns's reply is, "Oh, Mother Nature needs a favor does she? She should've thought of that when she was bombarding us with droughts and plagues and poison monkeys! Mother Nature started the war for survival, and now she wants to quit because she's losing? Well I say 'hard cheese.'" When Lisa balks at his war on nature, Mr. Burns says, "Surely, you agree we can do without her."

Mr. Burns's view epitomizes the most extreme version of what Spinoza would call treating humans as a "kingdom within a kingdom." In this case, though, Mr. Burns treats humans as if they were utterly separate from nature and not dependent on it in any way. His viewpoint reaches the height of absurdity when in order to regain his lost fortune he starts a "recycling" business of his own. At the heart of this business is the "Burns omni-net" made from plastic six-pack holders. The Burns omni-net "sweeps the sea clean" and the contents of the sea are then "recycled" into Li'l Lisa Slurry. "I call our product, Li'l Lisa's patented animal slurry. It's a high-protein feed for farm animals, insulation for low-income housing, a powerful explosive and a top-notch engine coolant," Mr. Burns explains. "And best of all, it's made from one hundred percent recycled animals!" Spinoza has already shown the ethical difficulties with supposing that humans are a kingdom within a kingdom, but such a view also raises problems for the environment.

No one is so callous or clueless to suppose that we have no relation to the environment. No one thinks that we can destroy natural resources with impunity. At the same time, however, to the degree that we suppose that humans operate by different rules than the rest of the universe, we are in danger of repeating Mr. Burns's mistakes on varying scales. If, conversely, we are able to think humanity as part of nature rather than opposed to it on some level, we begin to see ourselves differently and as a result treat the environment differently. In this final chapter I would like to examine how Spinoza might help us think through some of the environmental concerns that currently weigh so heavily on us.

The first step in thinking through these concerns is clarifying exactly where Spinoza's view differs from the widely held oppositional view. As we have already seen, for Spinoza it is impossible to think of a universe that operates on two fundamentally opposed sets of rules. We cannot imagine that the whole universe operates on the necessary relation of cause and effect, while humans are not bound by this natural causality. The reason most people assume that their will is free with regard to antecedent causes is simply ignorance of those causes. Giving support to this ignorance, however, is a philosophical doctrine known as "essentialism." We examined essentialism briefly in regard to the mind and also in regard to bodies. I'd like to take up that analysis again in order to show how it fosters the kind of attitude brilliantly satirized by *The Simpsons*.

Essentialism posits the existence of transcendent "essences" that define what an entity is, but at the same time do not undergo change along with the entity. Thus, essences are universal and ahistorical. The classic example of essentialism is found in Plato's theory of forms. Plato argues that knowledge would be impossible without something to ground that knowledge. We could not know what a chair was unless we had some prior knowledge of the essence of chair, chairness, under which any particular instance might be subsumed. Regular, everyday chairs are wildly varied and subject to constant change. How could we ever organize our thoughts, or even speak coherently, without some way to tame this confusion of chairs? Plato argues that true knowledge is not knowledge of particular chairs. There is too much variability here. Rather, true knowledge must lie in what does not change: the essence of chair, the form of chair, chairness itself. In order to ensure the purity of essence, (Insert your own *Dr. Strangelove* joke here.) Plato supposes that there is a separate and unchanging realm of essences safe from the corruption of change and decay. At the same time, the realm of corruption and decay (everyday life) reflects, participates in, shadows the realm of the forms.

The kind of dualism that Plato espouses gets taken up in numerous ways in the history of philosophy. We've already seen an echo of this dualism in Descartes, who argues that the mind is the essence of a person and the body is a mechanical appendage. Kant also argues for an irreducible dualism that traverses everything as the distinction between phenomena (appearance) and noumena (reality). What lies at the heart of all of these is an attempt to clean up the messiness of the world by stabilizing it in some realm that lies outside of the world, or at least is not subject to the vicissitudes of the changing world.

The danger of this viewpoint from the perspective of the environment is that it fosters precisely the kind of insular thinking that leads to an opposition between humans and nature. Essentialism requires one to think an object without reference to its connections. Thus, if we define the human essence, as Descartes does, as "a thing that thinks" we are left with a thinking thing without any definite or necessary thoughts. We are left with a thing with no necessary connection to its environment. On this model, Descartes is required to deduce the existence of the world external to the mind. However, since the self-enclosed mind is his starting point, he doesn't quite make it. He says we can deduce with certainty the *essence* of the external world (i.e., mathematics), but we cannot deduce with certainty the *existence* of the external world. Thus, while the essence of the world as mathematical can be deduced with certainty, we can only have a high degree of probability with regard to the existence of the external world. Suddenly, the idea that my mind, which I know with certainty, operates according to a different set of rules from the rest of the universe, which I only know with probability, becomes much more plausible.

This condition is exacerbated when we expand the same kind of essentialist thinking to plants, animals, and ecosystems. If I think about living organisms in terms of their essences, as Linnaean taxonomy encourages, then I will begin to think of species as static entities that can be wielded to solve problems. This kind of thinking is the reason that the Southeastern United States is drowning in kudzu. It's the reason that African honeybees were imported to South America and are now becoming an increasing problem in the United States. It's the reason that cane toads have taken over Northeastern Australia. Cane toads, for example, are known for their ability to eat large amounts of insects. As a result, they were imported from Central and South America to control the greyback cane beetle. The cane toad, however, brought more than its appetite. It brought a poison that was deadly to the native species of Australia. The predators that would normally keep a toad population in check were nowhere to be found. As a result, the population of cane toads exploded, which in turn further displaced other native species that occupied the same ecological niche. The definition of the cane toad as the eradicator of pests failed to take into account its relation with its environment and assumed that its effects would be the same regardless of the environment.

On the essentialist model the environment does not play an active role in shaping individuals or species. Individuals are simply manifestations of species, and species are defined in terms of an unchanging, transcendent essence. The environment becomes merely an empty space within which essences play out their roles. Each species is a hermetically sealed bubble that can be bumped but not changed by the other bubbles floating around. If an essence is that which must remain unchanged for any object to be itself, it is not surprising that we would not think holistically about what is true for all essences. By the same token, we could just as easily assume that each essence might operate according to its own laws.

Essentialism is also reductionist. This has been borne out repeatedly in terms of our relation to food. Either directly or indirectly, all of our food is dependent on plants, and plants are dependent on the soil. Obviously some soil is better for growing than others, and even this depends on what's being grown. The seemingly obvious solution is to ask what is it that makes soil good for growing, what makes it fertile. The answer to this question comes in the nineteenth century in the form of three letters N, P, and K. The essence of soil fertility is reduced to three chemical components nitrogen, phosphorus, and potassium. As our ability to produce these chemicals synthetically has increased, our crop productivity has increased exponentially. Isn't this increased productivity, though, a clear indication that essentialism works? Yes and no. No one can deny that we're now feeding more people than ever using these techniques. The problem is that these techniques have made us utterly dependent on petroleum, which is used to produce and transport these chemicals. Furthermore, the increased fertility comes at the price of reducing the amount of nutrients in the soil and the food grown from it. Finally, fields fertilized in this way create runoff that is changing both water and the plants near such fields. Essentialist thinking thrives on precisely this kind of reductive analysis that seems to provide solutions in the short term, but in the long term is unsustainable.[1]

Nutrition suffers a similar fate to soil fertility. Initially, it was thought that human nutrition was dependent on the macronutrients: carbohydrates, proteins, and fats. Eventually, however, it was discovered the macronutrients were insufficient to prevent diseases like scurvy or beri beri. There must be more to the story than macronutrients, namely micronutrients, such as vitamins and minerals. Scurvy and beri beri are the result of vitamin deficiencies. The thinking that has followed from this discovery has led to a never-ending parade of heroes and villains. All fats are bad, but carbs are good. Some fats are good, but carbs are bad. Get more vitamin C in your diet. Fiber is the new C. Omega-3 fatty acids are the new fiber. On and on it goes. The reductionist assumption that there is a one-to-one correspondence between a particular nutrient and a desired effect, however, goes unquestioned. Omega-3 fatty acids are supposed to lower the risk of coronary heart disease, for example. The result is that anchovies get pureed into everything from orange juice to rye bread so that it can be labeled "heart healthy." Unfortunately, human nutrition is much more complicated than this. It may in fact be the case that it's not omega-3s *per se*, but the ratio of omega-3 fatty acids to omega-6 fatty acids. This is not something that can be discovered, though, if nutrition science insists on looking at individual nutrients for a miracle cure.[2] Thus, analogously to soil fertility, the advances of nutrition science cannot be denied, but because it is essentialist, it has reached the limits imposed on it by its methodology. Nutrition science is very good at discovering when diseases arise from a nutrition deficiency, but not as good with the very mundane question, what should one eat?

As we have seen, Spinoza's response to the essentialism that dominates the history of philosophy is to focus on particulars rather than "universals." By particulars Spinoza has in mind the specific properties of individuals. This allows Spinoza a much richer description of the world, since he is not required to lop off any extraneous properties that do not fit on the Procrustean bed of the "universal." Instead, Spinoza argues that our knowledge advances when we understand how these properties interact with other properties according to necessary laws. This allows us to define individuals according to what they can do. What an individual can do, of course, is dependent on two factors, its affects and the degree to which it exercises those affects. This view of the individual makes the reductionism inherent in essentialism impossible, because it requires us to think the individual not only as a set of properties but also the exercise of those properties. An individual is defined in terms of a ratio of motion and rest, slowness and speeds. The individual thus becomes inseparable from its relations to the world. No essentialist hermeticism is possible here, because the individual cannot be defined apart from the particular way it is exercising its affects at this moment.

We have seen how this view affects Spinoza's ethics. Let's turn to how it affects his views of the environment. One of Spinoza's commentators puts it this way:

> Every point has its counterpoints: the plant and the rain, the spider and the fly. So an animal, a thing, is never separable from its relations with the world. The interior is only a selected exterior, and the exterior, a projected interior. The speed or slowness of metabolisms, perceptions, actions, and reactions link together to constitute a particular individual in the world."[3]

It is impossible to define an individual in isolation from its environment. The individual is nothing but a temporary coagulation of materials drawn from the environment in a particular ratio. This ratio, which determines what is poisonous and what is healthful, what is predator and what is prey, cannot be determined outside of the very specificity of the environment. As we have seen, to define a creature in isolation from these relations is to court disaster, as in the case of kudzu, African honey bees, and cane toads. Often these transplants fail because they cannot interact with their new environment in the same way as their old environment. What was healthy is now harmful, and hitherto unknown predators feast on an unexpected food source.

The environment is a systemic series of mutually interdependent individuals, and by replacing essentialism Spinoza gives us the tools for thinking the systematicity of nature. For Spinoza everything is an individual of this type, it is only a question of scale. One can think the smallest single-celled organism as a ratio of motion and rest and one can think about the earth as a whole as an infinitely complex ratio of motion and rest. Regardless of the scale, though, one cannot expect to transplant an individual from one local system to another without consequence. Individual and environment go together like a lock and key. Ultimately, one cannot even rigorously distinguish between the individual and the environment. Each is the other seen from a different scale. The environment is shaped by its component parts just as much as the parts are shaped by the environment. The barrier between individual and environment predicated on essentialist thinking becomes untenable, and one begins to think only in terms of individuals as ratios of motion and rest that are necessarily exercising their affects to some degree.

From Spinoza's perspective all thinking is "environmental" and not limited to a way of thinking about ecosystems. Just as there is no sharp distinction between the individual and its environment, there is also no sharp distinction between the natural and the artificial.[4] Such a distinction returns us to the problem of essentialism. Rather, Spinoza proposes that we think everything, whether made by humans or by natural processes and regardless of scale, as a particular ratio of motion and rest. The primary concern is not its origin, but what it can do. Furthermore, everything is part of the same nature and interacts with it in some way. It's only on this view that we can begin to ask questions such as: How do petroleum-based fertilizers affect water supplies? Are CO_2 emissions having an effect on average temperatures? Are genetically modified crops a potential danger to humans, animals, or the environment? Is industrial agriculture's dependence on monocultures for high production yields a source of concern? All of these questions (and many others) can only be properly answered if we think systemically and in telescopic scales of mutually interdependent individuals.

It's thinking in these terms that have led some to hail Spinoza as a patron saint of the environmental movement, particularly what's known as "deep ecology." There are some, however, who balk at Spinoza's inclusion. What concerns them in particular is Spinoza's claims about animals. Spinoza writes:

> [T]he law against killing animals is based more on empty superstition and unmanly compassion than sound reason. The rational principle of seeking our own advantage teaches us the necessity of joining with men, but not with the lower animals, or with things whose nature is different from human nature. We have the same right against them that they have against us. Indeed because the right of each one is defined by his virtue, or power, men have a far greater right against the lower animals than they have against men. Not that I deny that the lower animals have sensations. But I do deny that we are therefore not permitted to consider our own advantage, use them at our pleasure, and treat them as is most convenient for us. For they do not agree in nature with us, and their affects are different in nature from human affects.[5]

As we saw in the chapter on Spinoza's politics nothing is more useful to us than other people. The reason for this is that the more something agrees with our nature, the more our combining with it increases our power. In the case of other people, insofar as perfect agreement is possible, the power increase is double. In contrast to this, animals are not so constituted that they can fully agree with our nature. Their ways of affecting and being affected are fundamentally different from ours. Spinoza concludes two things from this. First, since their ways of affecting and being affected are different, their natures are different, and therefore they cannot be as useful to us as other people. This first conclusion seems un-problematic. Humans are different from animals (although as we've seen, the dif-ference is not one of essence or substance), and so we can't interact with them in the same way. The second conclusion, however, seems much more problematic. Spinoza reasons that because animals can't be as useful to us as other people it is our "right" to treat them in a way that is beneficial to us.

Part of the difficulty arises from Spinoza's use of the term "right." We gen-erally tend to think of rights as something that's due us by virtue of our being human, such as life, liberty, and the pursuit of happiness. These rights cannot be taken away for any reason, and it is the government's duty to defend these rights in us. A government that fails in this duty is rightly overthrown and replaced with a government that can fulfill its duty. As we've seen, and as the quote makes ex-plicit here, Spinoza does not have this conception of right in mind. He says flatly that right, virtue, and power are all equivalent expressions. This model allows Spinoza to make two seemingly opposed claims: 1) We have the same rights over animals that they have over us, and 2) We have greater rights over animals than they have over us. How can these two claims be reconciled? I take the first claim to be a generic claim about power. Everything everywhere expresses its power in keeping with its ratio of motion and rest. This is what Spinoza calls "striving." When two individuals collide, either one will overcome the other, or to the degree that their natures coincide, the individuals will combine into a new more pow-erful individual. The first claim is, then, about the physics of collisions. In any collision only a few basic outcomes are possible, and these outcomes follow from the "right" or power of the individuals involved. It is in this sense that our rights and animal rights are equivalent. The second claim involves a more specific claim about human nature, namely, that a human individual is more complex than an animal individual. As a result, the human individual is capable of affecting and begin affected in more ways than the animal individual. This is the source of hu-man power, virtue, or right. From this perspective, humans have more rights over animals than animals have over them.

When we overlook Spinoza's use of the term "right" and instead import the traditional definition of "right," we force him into saying something that he is not. On this traditional reading Spinoza's claim becomes "humans occupy a higher place on the ladder of being than animals; we can therefore mistreat them in any way we wish," which in turn seems to justify any torture or cruelty we wish to dish out. In opposition to this position attributed to Spinoza, some would argue that the only way to avoid wanton cruelty toward animals is to affirm the rights of animals in the same way that we affirm the rights of humans. Animals also have an inherent right to life, liberty, and the pursuit of happiness. To deny animals these rights is to deny them their nature. From Spinoza's perspective this position rests on a profound confusion about rights and the nature of the universe itself. To begin with, arguing for human rights in the traditional sense supposes an essentialist reading of human nature. Furthermore, it supposes that humans are a kingdom within a kingdom, operating according to laws that differ from the laws of nature. Finally, a discourse on animal rights that bestows the same kind of rights on animals that it does on humans simply expands the domain of the kingdom within a kingdom to include both humans and animals.

Spinoza is, of course, trying to think our relation to animals without resorting to either essentialism or its correlate—the kingdom within a kingdom. The result is that he sees all of nature as an infinitely complex system of individuals relating to individuals and in that relating some combine with others, while some decompose others. Within this context he notes that we *do* have the ability to kill other animals, and that there is nothing in the laws of the universe to prevent this or universally proscribe it. At the same time, Spinoza always returns us to the fundamental question of the source of our actions. Do our actions result from a combination with external causes, or do our actions follow necessarily from our nature alone? Are we active or passive? Free or in bondage?

Spinoza's philosophy does not allow for a simple prescriptive answer here, which will undoubtedly make it of no value for champions of a traditional conception of animal rights. At the same time, it does allow us to ask experimental questions about the nature and particularly the source of our food. The twentieth century saw the rise of factory farms and the use of industrial methods for producing meat, poultry, and dairy. Access to cheap sources of protein undoubtedly improved things like decreasing infant mortality and increasing the average height of adults. It also saw a rise in heart disease and obesity-related illness, not to mention the degradation of the environment as a result of concentrated holding areas and slaughter practices. Given these, and numerous other complicating factors, Spinoza would ask if this is the only way to relate to our food supply. Is there a way to relate to our food such that we maintain the benefits without the detriments? Answering this question will require a broad rethinking on an environmental scale that takes into account the systematic interdependence of all the individuals, human, animal, plant, and water systems, involved.

NOTES

1. For an expanded treatment of these issues see Michael Pollan's *The Omnivore's Dilemma: A Natural History of Four Meals* (New York: Penguin, 2007), and *In Defense of Food: An Eater's Manifesto* (New York: Penguin, 2008).
2. Pollan, *In Defense of Food*, 31ff.
3. Deleuze, *Spinoza: Practical Philosophy*, 125.
4. Deleuze, *Spinoza: Practical Philosophy*, 124.
5. IVP37S1.

Conclusion:
How to Become a
Spinozist in Three Easy Steps

As a practical guide to Spinoza's philosophy, I have argued that his philosophy provides an account of how we might live. The "might" here stands in contradistinction to accounts of how we *should* live or how we *should* act. Spinoza thus provides a descriptive ethics rather than a prescriptive one. Spinoza's fundamental ethical insight lies in the fact that understanding gives us power over the emotions. Or, as we saw in the case of road rage, to the degree that I understand I cannot be angry. As we progressed through Spinoza's thought we saw that this intuition has a very broad application. It led us to a general theory of affecting and being affected, to an account of the relation between mind and body, to a full-blown unified theory of everything. It was only at this point that we could understand what Spinoza meant by freedom. True freedom has nothing to do with free will for Spinoza. True freedom is acting in accord with who one is, being oneself, not being controlled by external causes opposed to one's nature. Once we understood what Spinoza meant by freedom we could move on to issues that, although larger in scale, involved the same fundamental dynamics: politics, religion, and the environment. Again the criterion for analyzing these large conglomerations of humans and humans with non-human aspects of the universe remains freedom. Spinoza remains adamant that those combinations that increase our ways of affecting and being affected, (i.e., those that promote rather than hinder human striving, power, or virtue) are to be pursued, and those that decrease it are to be avoided.

What I would like to do by way of conclusion, then, is to summarize the practicality of Spinoza's position as three formulas that characterize the path of wisdom.

THIS COULD NOT BE OTHERWISE

The source of all folly for Spinoza lies in assuming that things could have been different from what they are. To insinuate contingency into the nature of the universe is simply to project our own ignorance onto the universe and make it into a fundamental principle of human nature. This was precisely the problem in the case of road rage from the first chapter. My hatred and anger stemmed from the fact that I assumed that the driver of the SUV could have acted otherwise. When I discovered the reasons for his actions, my guilt and shame also stemmed from the fact that I assumed that I could have acted otherwise. It is only when I realize that nothing could have been other than it is that I cease to be controlled by causes external to me and in opposition to my nature. Spinoza states this principle very clearly when he says,

> He who rightly knows that all things follow from the necessity of the divine nature, and happen according to the eternal laws and rules of nature, will surely find nothing worthy of hate, mockery or disdain, nor anyone whom he will pity. Instead he will strive, as far as human virtue allows, to act well, as they say, and rejoice.[1]

Some would argue that this simply reaffirms the *status quo*. There is no reason to pursue change, if everything happens of necessity. Furthermore, this destroys both the foundations of morality and the basis of our legal system, which depend on the notion that one always could have acted otherwise. The first objection confuses Spinoza's determinist position with fatalism or predestination. It assumes that everything that happens was meant to be, usually in order to fulfill some greater purpose. What fatalism and predestination both suppose, though, that Spinoza's position does not is there is some set end point, some final cause toward which we are inexorably heading. Thus, Oedipus's parents in an effort to avoid their fate send Oedipus away, which leads to the same end that Oedipus kills his father and marries his mother. Both fate and predestination say that the path one walks down is irrelevant, because it will eventually reach the one predetermined endpoint. Spinoza's position, however, does not depend on a predetermined end for any individual or the universe as a whole. Rather, Spinoza's position is that our current choices are determined by previous causes. In Spinoza one gets the sense that we are being driven from behind rather than being led to some final point. Nothing in Spinoza's position suggests that we have a fate that we will meet no matter which path we travel down. Rather, his position suggests that every choice we make can teach us. Where that leads us is unpredictable, but this is not the same thing as saying that our choices are therefore freely made.

To the second objection, Spinoza would unapologetically say that he is trying to refound the entire system of human ethics and along with it our politics. On Spinoza's model, ethics cannot be founded on a kind of responsibility that presupposes free will. It's precisely for this reason that he proposes a descriptive rather than a prescriptive ethics. Spinoza excludes the judge as a model for ethics or even for God. Virtue is its own reward, and vice is its own punishment; in the same way that health is the reward for eating well and sickness is the reward for consuming poison. Does this mean that we should open all the prisons, since no one is responsible for his or her actions (in the sense that none could have acted otherwise)? No, but the goal of criminal justice does become different. It would be absurd on Spinoza's view to punish someone because he could have acted otherwise. At the same time, it is not absurd to suppose that a state might instigate measures to ensure that those who act against the common interest might learn not to do so in the future. These measures might not be imprisonment. Again, Spinoza would think it strange to have a one-size-fits-all method of rehabilitation. It seems as if he would favor rehabilitation that's calibrated to the individual.

What I am proposing here is an experiment in practical Spinozism. Try it for yourself and see if it works. No matter what happens, say to yourself, "This could not be otherwise," and see what happens to your mood. See if you are less or more affected by causes opposed to your nature. See if your thoughts become more your own or are continually sidetracked by external thoughts that intrude on you. In short, see if this makes you more or less free. It seems very clear to me what would've happened if, instead of flying into an impotent rage when I was cut off by the SUV, I simply said, "This could not be otherwise." I would've remained myself. I wouldn't have found anything worthy of "hate, mockery or disdain." I would've been free.

UNDERSTANDING THINGS IN THEIR PARTICULARITY

While understanding the necessity of things animated the first half of the book, understanding things in their particularity animated the second half. In addition to the difficulties caused by the presupposition of free will in humans and contingency in the universe, another kind of conceptual problem arises from thinking in terms of "universals." I've used the scare quotes throughout in order to highlight that, although this way of thinking attempts to get at what is real and essential, it fails because it abstracts from the properties of things and makes claims about chair-ness or dog-ness or humanness.

In contrast to this Spinoza proposes a radically fine-grained approach to knowledge. He argues that each individual is radically unique and to speak of anything as an instance of a universal obscures more than it reveals. The fine-grained approach is adjustable in terms of scale. Individuals can be thought of on a very small or a very large scale, but this thinking must not obscure the particularity of the individual. To this end, Spinoza argues that we must not think of individuals in terms of essence or substance, but in terms of a ratio of motion and rest among its parts. This ratio makes certain ways of affecting and being affected possible, and these affects will be exercised to a certain degree. It's in terms of these coordinates that we get the best understanding of what an individual can do.

Initially, the results of this kind of understanding seem strange. As one commentator noted, it would require us to think that the plow horse has more in common with an ox than a race horse. Our hesitancy here, though, follows from the essentialist presuppositions of our own thinking. What Spinoza's way of thinking opens up, though, are entire new vistas of thinking across boundaries or transversally. We might fruitfully explore the relation between a steam-engine and a hurricane or between the self-organizing forces of geological formations and the way cities form.[2] When we are no longer bound by "universals" we can begin looking at how properties interact with one another, and we might discover that properties in supposedly radically heterogeneous domains have a great deal in common.

The greatest boon that understanding things in their particularity provides, though, is it allows us to think systemically, environmentally. Everything for Spinoza is in constant interaction with everything around it. This system of affecting and being affected can itself be studied as a ratio of motion and rest that makes ways of affecting and being affected possible and which are exercised to a certain degree. The sharp distinction between individual and environment disappears. Individuals are no longer hermetically sealed and cannot be understood apart from their environment. The environment can no longer be seen as a blank slate on which different essences interact. The distinction between human or animal and environment on Spinoza's model becomes one of scale. The fundamental principles hold regardless of the scale. Spinoza argues strenuously that everyone and everything operates according to the same rules. There are no kingdoms within kingdoms in Spinoza's universe.

NO ONE KNOWS WHAT A BODY CAN DO

I have argued throughout that Spinoza's ethics is first and foremost an experimentalism. This follows from the fact that his ethics are descriptive rather than prescriptive. This might seem to be at odds, though, with Spinoza's determinism. If our actions are determined by prior causes is experimentation even possible? And, if it is, what is our motivation for experimenting? Again, it is important not to confuse determinism with there being a set endpoint to our lives. Seeing the value in experimentation could itself be a cause that would determine us to pursue more experimentation. The motivation for experimentation comes from Spinoza's claims about understanding necessity and the importance of the individual. He writes, "Whatever so disposes the human body that it can be affected in a great many ways, or renders it capable of affecting bodies in a great many ways, is useful."[3] The more we engage with things in their particularity and the more particulars we engage with, the more we are able to understand. The more we are able to understand the more we are able to see the necessity in things, and thus the more we are able to be free with regard to them rather than in bondage.

Furthermore, this is the kind of understanding that can only come through experience. Spinoza is often caricatured as a hyper-rationalist who believes that everything can be deduced a priori, prior to experience. Given that the mind is not separate from the body, but simply one of two stories we can tell about the same individual, there wouldn't be a mind operating independently of the body. There would only be an individual's ways of affecting and being affected and the two accounts one could give. From Spinoza's perspective this view necessitates that one interact with the world to know anything at all. Spinoza says it this way, "For indeed, no one has yet determined what the body can do, i.e., experience has not yet taught anyone what the body can do from the laws of nature alone."[4] The human body is incredibly complex, which makes it capable of a great number of affects. The number is so great, in fact, that one cannot know what a body can do without actually experimenting with it. So, on the one hand, Spinoza can say in general that whatever decomposes a body's ratio of motion and rest is harmful to it. On the other hand, he cannot say that every cause will have the same effect on every body. Spinoza's anti-essentialism prevents him from making these kinds of claims. His only recourse is to say, "Try it and see." The more things you try the more you will understand what your body is capable of, and the more you will understand what is poisonous and what is healthy for you. Thus, it is only by experimenting that one can see the path of wisdom.

The political implications of Spinoza's experimentalism are far-reaching. In order for a state to be constituted so that it opens up rather than limiting possibilities for affecting and being affected, the state must be one that ensures freedom of thought and freedom of speech. The state's health and stability, the maintenance of *its* ratio of motion and rest, is in fact dependent on safeguarding these freedoms. A state without these freedoms would retard the ability of individuals in the state to combine with other things—especially other people—that would be useful to them. This inability would prevent individuals from understanding themselves and the world, which would make them less virtuous, less powerful. The lack of power in the constituent parts of the state, the individuals, would in turn lead to the diminution of the state's power. Eventually, the state's cohesion would fail. It would be unable to maintain its ratio of motion and rest. It would no longer be capable of the same affects. As a result, Spinoza argues that the state as a whole must engage in a kind of experimentalism through maintaining avenues of exploration for its members.

The religious implications of Spinoza's experimentalism are equally far-reaching. The great danger to freedom is superstition. Superstition creates a (literally from Spinoza's perspective) vicious circle in which people bemoan the susceptibility to the changing tides of history, bad luck, and seek to protect themselves from it in any way possible. Under the false belief that their lives could have been otherwise they begin to engage in magical thinking about the way the universe works. Suddenly, ordinary objects take on power far beyond their causal efficacy.

Rituals become imbued with outsized significance, all in an effort to interrupt the necessary connection of cause and effect. Superstition is precisely the kind of bondage that Spinoza seeks to free us from. Superstition replaces understanding the necessity and particularity of things with a partial and inadequate understanding of the world based on the imagination rather than reason. Superstition also forestalls experimentation. Not only is my engagement with the world predicated on false assumptions in superstition, but it also forecloses on avenues of exploration. If I think, for example, that illness is caused by demons intervening in human affairs supernaturally, I will seek to cure that illness through supernatural means rather than seeking its source in the necessary laws of nature.

Superstition is even more dangerous, though, when it becomes institutionalized. In its institutional form superstition is supported by hope and fear. Again, as we have seen, hope and fear are no less forms of bondage than superstition. What hope and fear do for superstition is to colonize the future by extending the effects of superstition indefinitely. Hope and fear become the carrot and stick that guide us solely on the path laid out by the superstition. I run from the bad effects of not following the superstition, and I run toward the good future effect promised by following the superstition. I am also supported in this path by everyone else who follows the same superstition. Thus, the superstition's hold on me grows, and I become less free, less able to experiment with the world beyond these bounds.

Having said all of this, it's important to note that Spinoza is not anti-religious. In the same way that he thinks the only way to stabilize the state is through freedom, the only way to preserve piety is by eliminating superstition. Any act done out of hope or fear is not virtuous. It indicates the act of someone in bondage. Piety, true love of God and humanity, can only arise out of freedom, not out of superstition. True freedom is only possible to the degree that we understand the necessity and particularity of the universe in order to experiment with our incredibly complex ways of affecting and being affected.

In closing, I'd like to return to a section that we looked at briefly in chapter 1. This is the conclusion to Spinoza's *Ethics*, and, I think, one of the most edifying passages in the history of philosophy.

> From what has been shown, it is clear how much the wise man is capable of, and how much more powerful he is than one who is ignorant and is driven only by lust. For not only is the ignorant man troubled in many ways by external causes, and unable ever to possess true peace of mind, but he also lives as if he knew neither himself, nor God, nor things; and as soon as he ceases to be acted on, he ceases to be. On the other hand, the wise man, insofar as he is considered as such, is hardly troubled in spirit, but being, by a certain eternal necessity, conscious of himself, and of God, and of things, he never ceases to be, but always possesses true peace of mind.
>
> If the way I have shown to lead to these things now seems very hard, still, it can be found. And of course, what is found so rarely must be hard. For if salvation were at hand, and could be found without great effort, how could nearly everyone neglect it? But all things excellent are as difficult as they are rare.[5]

Initially, we looked at this passage simply in terms of its opposition between the wise and the ignorant and compared to similar passages drawn from the wisdom literature of the Hebrew Bible. Now, we can see how nicely it summarizes the entirety of Spinoza's practical philosophy. Wisdom lies in understanding oneself, God, and things. This kind of understanding can only come through seeing things in their particularity and necessity. The result of this kind of understanding is "peace of mind." Freedom from the bondage of external causes makes possible the freedom to be oneself. The path of wisdom is not easily traveled. Giving up engrained notions like free will and "universals" takes patience and practice, but the rewards far outweigh the costs.

NOTES

1. IVP50S.
2. Manuel DeLanda does precisely this in *A Thousand Years of Nonlinear History* (New York: Zone Publishing, 1997).
3. IVP38.
4. IIIP2S.
5. VP42S.

Bibliography

Brennan, Teresa. *The Transmission of Affect*. Ithaca, N.Y.: Cornell University Press, 2004.

Damasio, Antonio. *Looking for Spinoza: Joy, Sorrow, and the Feeling Brain*. New York: Harcourt, Inc., 2003.

DeLanda, Manuel. *A New Philosophy of Society: Assemblage Theory and Social Complexity*. New York: Continuum, 2006.

———. *A Thousand Years of Nonlinear History*. New York: Zone Publishing, 1997.

Deleuze, Gilles. *Spinoza: Practical Philosophy*. Translated by Robert Hurley. San Francisco: City Lights, 1988.

Foucault, Michel. *The Hermeneutics of Subject: Lectures at the Collège de France, 1981–1982*. Translated by Graham Burchell. New York: Picador, 2005.

Locke, John. *Essay Concerning Human Understanding* in *The Empiricists*. New York: Doubleday, 1961.

Malamud, Bernard. *The Fixer*. New York: Farrar, Straus, and Giroux, 2004.

May, Todd. *Gilles Deleuze: An Introduction*. New York: Cambridge University Press, 2005.

New American Standard Bible. Nashville, Tenn.: Holman Bible Publishers, 1977.

Pollan, Michael. *In Defense of Food: An Eater's Manifesto.* New York: Penguin, 2008.

————. *The Collected Works of Spinoza, vol. 1.* Edited and translated by Edwin Curley. Princeton: Princeton University Press, 1985.

————. *The Omnivore's Dilemma: A Natural History of Four Meals.* New York: Penguin, 2007.

Spinoza, Baruch. *Spinoza: Complete Works.* Translated by Samuel Shirley. Indianapolis: Hackett Publishing, 2002.

Wolfson, Harry Austryn. *The Philosophy of Spinoza.* New York: Schocken Books, 1969.

Index

active, 1, 9, 16, 19–20, 23, 28, 36, 43–45, 52, 85, 90. *See also* passive
affects, 7–9, 14–20, 21, 24–28, 32, 35–36, 38, 44, 49–50, 52, 56–62, 63–64, 66–67, 69–70, 73, 75–76, 79, 87–89, 91, 93–96. *See also* emotions
anger, 6–7, 27–28, 40, 47, 50–52, 68, 79–80, 92. *See also* affects, emotions
Aristotle, 2, 9, 18–19, 22, 30, 33
attribute, 32–35, 39–40, 42, 44, 55, 63, 77

blessedness (*beatitudo*), 52, 76. *See also* freedom
Blijenbergh, Willem van, 59–60, 73, 77
body, 14–15, 30–32, 37–40, 42, 46, 55–58, 62–64, 68, 76–77, 80, 84, 91, 94–95. *See also* extension, matter
bondage, 12, 25–29, 36, 44–45, 51, 59, 61, 77, 80, 90, 95–97
Buddhism, 1

causality, 8, 10, 15–20, 24–28, 29, 31, 34–36, 39–41, 44–46, 48, 51–52, 61, 66–67, 69, 74–77, 79, 84, 90, 91–97
chaos theory, 35–36
Christianity, 9, 73–75, 78
common notions, 42
completion. *See* perfection

Deleuze, Gilles, 11–12, 62n4, 62n6, 90n3, 90n4
democracy, 70
Descartes, René, 7, 30–32, 37–40, 84–85
dualism. *See* substance

emotions, 1, 3, 6–7, 14–15, 18, 26, 32, 52, 57, 66, 91. *See also* affects
environment, 1, 7, 11–12, 42, 55, 58, 61–62, 83–85, 87–90, 91, 94
Epicureanism, 9
epistemology, 2, 37
essence/essentialism, 19, 30–32, 35, 43, 59–60, 66, 75, 84–90, 93–95
eternality, 8, 44, 52, 76–77, 80, 92, 96
ethics, 2–3, 6, 8–12, 14–15, 28, 50, 59–61, 64, 70, 76, 84, 87, 91–94; consequentialism, 10; deontology, 10; descriptive, 9–12, 60, 80, 91, 94; experimental, 11–12, 58, 90, 94–95; prescriptive, 9–12, 60, 90–91, 93–94; relativism, 59–61
extension, 31, 34, 37–40, 42, 44, 55, 63. *See also* matter, thought

fatalism, 92, 102–103
fear, 8, 42, 66–68, 79–80, 96. *See also* hope, superstition
Foucault, Michel, 11

101

freedom, 1, 2, 3, 4, 11, 26, 45–52, 55, 58–59, 65–70, 73, 76–77, 80–81, 84, 90–93, 95–97; of speech, 68–69, 95; of the will 46–50, 59, 91–93, 97; of thought, 70, 95

God, 7–9, 20, 29–30, 34, 43, 73–79, 81, 93, 96–97
Greenspan, Alan, 63
Groundhog Day, 47–48

habit, 11, 22–25, 27, 48, 50–51
Hampshire, Stuart, 2
hate, 8, 17–18, 25, 52, 61, 63, 65, 92–93. *See also* affects, emotions
Hegel, G.W.F., 65
Hobbes, Thomas, 65–66
hope, 79–80, 96. *See also* fear, superstition
human rights, 65–66, 76, 88–90. *See also* power, virtue

immortality. *See* eternality
infinite, 33, 43, 51, 74–76, 87, 90
intuitive knowledge, 43–44, 52, 75, 81. *See also* mind, thought

joy (*laetitia*), 16–19, 24, 26–27, 59, 75–76, 79. *See also* affects, emotions
Judaism, 1, 9, 74
judgment, 1, 10–11, 61, 70, 76, 79, 93

Kant, Immanuel, 2, 10, 65, 84

Levinas, Emmanuel, 2
Locke, John, 49–50, 65
love, 13–15, 17–18, 24–25, 66, 73–76, 78–79, 96. *See also* affects, emotions

Malamud, Bernard, 3
matter, 37–40. *See also* mind
metaphysics, 2, 33, 36, 57, 77
Mill, J.S., 2
mind, 7–9, 16–17, 20, 22, 24, 28, 30–32, 36, 37–44, 46, 49–50, 52, 55, 59, 75–77, 80, 84–85, 87, 89, 91, 95–97
mode, 32, 36, 76, 78
monism. *See* substance

mood, 63, 93. *See also* affects
morality, 6, 10–11, 22, 46–47, 50, 59, 80, 92. *See also* ethics

necessity, 8, 10, 15, 19, 25, 35–36, 39–46, 48–52, 55, 58, 61, 65, 69, 73–78, 80–81, 84–85, 87–88, 90, 92–97
neuroscience, 55
Nietzsche, Friedrich, 2, 11, 12, 41

opinion, 41

pain, 39–41. *See also* affects
pantheism, 2, 29, 34, 74–76
passive, 1, 7–8, 16–17, 20, 24, 36, 44, 52, 77, 90. *See also* active
Paulson, Henry M., 67
perfection, 16–20, 24, 26, 33, 59, 75
piety, 69, 77–78, 80, 96. *See also* religion
Plato, 84
politics, 1, 3, 12, 62, 63–70, 73–74, 76, 79–80, 88, 91–92, 95
power, 12, 16, 18–19, 22, 24–25, 27, 49–52, 60, 64–68, 74–75, 88–89, 91, 95–96. *See also* virtue, right, striving
predestination. *See* fatalism
psychology, 12, 37

quantum mechanics, 35

ratio of motion and rest, 56–61, 64, 66–67, 70, 76, 87–89, 93–95. *See also* body, speeds and slowness
reason, 11, 19, 33, 42–44, 46, 66, 68, 70, 96. *See also* mind, thought
religion, 1, 3, 12, 62, 64, 73–74, 77–80, 91. See also piety
Rousseau, J.-J., 65

sadness (*tristitia*), 16–17, 19, 24, 26–27, 63, 66, 79. *See also* affects, emotions
Seinfeld: "The Kiss Hello," 23; "The Soup Nazi," 21, 23–27; "The Switch," 21
self, 11, 22–23
The Simpsons, 27; "The Old Man and the Lisa," 83–84; "The Springfield Files," 13, 18

social contract, 65–66. *See also* politics, state

speeds and slowness, 56, 87. *See also* body, ratio of motion and rest

state, 64–69, 73, 95–96. *See also* politics

Stoicism, 9, 26

striving (*conatus*), 16–20, 24, 26–27, 52, 89, 91–92. *See also* affects, emotions

substance, 2, 30–34, 36–39, 43, 56–57, 74, 76, 78, 89, 93

superstition, 79–80, 88, 95–96. *See also* fear, hope

thought, 7, 9, 27, 31–44, 46–47, 49–52, 55, 63, 76–77, 84–85, 93. *See also* mind

tick, 57–58, 60, 64

transversal, 42, 94

understanding, 1, 7–8, 14, 16–17, 19, 28–29, 33, 36, 44–45, 52, 55, 58, 60–62, 64–67, 75–77, 81, 91, 93–97. *See also* reason

universals, 42–44, 58, 61, 87, 93–94, 97. *See also* essence/essentialism

universe. *See* substance

vice, 14, 61, 65–66, 77, 93. *See also* bondage, virtue

virtue, 11, 52, 59–61, 65–66, 77, 80, 88–89, 91–93, 95–96

Printed in Great Britain
by Amazon